You and Me

Let's Do It Together

Denise M. Jordan

Heinemann Library
Chicago, Illinois

© 2004 Heinemann Library,
a division of Reed Elsevier, Inc.
Chicago, Illinois

Customer Service 888-454-2279
Visit our website at www.heinemannlibrary.com

Designed by Sue Emerson, Heinemann Library; Page layout by Que-Net Media™
Printed and bound in China by South China Printing Company Limited
Photo research by Janet Lankford Moran

08 07 06 05 04
10 9 8 7 6 5 4 3 2 1

Library of Congress Cataloging-in-Publication Data
Jordan, Denise.
   Let's do it together / Denise M. Jordan.
      p. cm. – (You and me)
Summary: Simple text and pictures explain when, where, why, and how we can help other people.
   ISBN 1-4034-4406-4 (HC), 1-4034-4412-9 (Pbk)
   1. Cooperativeness–Moral and ethical aspects–Juvenile literature.   2. Helping behavior–Juvenile literature.
[1. Cooperativeness. 2. Helpfulness.] I. Title.
   BJ1533.C74J67 2003
   177'.7–dc22

                                        2003012811

Acknowledgments
The author and publishers are grateful to the following for permission to reproduce copyright material:
pp. 4, 5, 16, 19 Myrleen Ferguson Cate/PhotoEdit Inc.; p. 6 Spencer Grant/PhotoEdit Inc.; pp. 7, 22, 24 Robert Lifson/ Heinemann Library; p. 8. Michael Keller/Corbis p. 9 Nancy Brown/Corbis; p. 10 Getty Images; p. 11 Corbis; pp. 12, 13, 14, 15 Que-Net/Heinemann Library; p. 17 Mary Kate Denny/PhotoEdit Inc.; p. 18 Ariel Skelley/Corbis; pp. 20, 21 Janet L. Moran/Oijoy Photography; p. 23 (T-B) Myrleen Ferguson Cate/PhotoEdit Inc., Myrleen Ferguson Cate/PhotoEdit Inc., Robert Lifson/Heinemann Library; back cover (L-R) Myrleen Ferguson Cate/PhotoEdit Inc., Que-Net/Heinemann Library

Cover photograph by Ariel Skelley/Corbis

Every effort has been made to contact copyright holders of any material reproduced in this book.
Any omissions will be rectified in subsequent printings if notice is given to the publisher.

Special thanks to our advisory panel for their help in the preparation of this book:
Alice Bethke, Library Consultant
Palo Alto, CA

Eileen Day, Preschool Teacher
Chicago, IL

Kathleen Gilbert,
Second Grade Teacher
Round Rock, TX

Sandra Gilbert,
Library Media Specialist
Fiest Elementary School
Houston, TX

Jan Gobeille,
Kindergarten Teacher
Garfield Elementary
Oakland, CA

Angela Leeper,
Educational Consultant
Wake Forest, NC

Some words are shown in bold, **like this.**
You can find them in the picture glossary on page 23.

Contents

What Is Helping?. 4

Where Can You Help? 6

Why Do You Help? 8

Who Can You Help?. 10

What Do You See When You Help?. . . 12

What Do You Hear When You Help?. . 14

How Can You Help at Home?. 16

How Can You Help in Your
     Neighborhood?. 18

How Do You Feel When You Help?. . . 20

Quiz. 22

Picture Glossary 23

Note to Parents and Teachers. 24

Answer to Quiz 24

Index 24

What Is Helping?

Helping is doing something for or with someone else.

When you help someone, you **cooperate**.

Sometimes you work with others when you help.

Together, you can get a job done.

Where Can You Help?

You can help at home.

You can help at school.

You can help in your neighborhood, too.

You can help in many places.

Why Do You Help?

You help because it is a good thing to do.

You help because someone needs you to help them.

People working together can get a job done faster.

Helping makes a hard job easier.

Who Can You Help?

You can help your brother learn how to tie his shoes.

You can show him how to make a bow.

You can help your mom.

You can help her with the dishes after dinner.

What Do You See When You Help?

You see smiling faces when you help.

People are happy when you help them.

You can see a job getting done.

Jobs get done faster when people work together.

What Do You Hear When You Help?

You may hear "Thank you."

People say, "Thank you," after someone has helped them.

If someone tells you, "Thank you,"
you should say, "You are welcome."

Saying "You are welcome," is the
polite thing to do.

How Can You Help at Home?

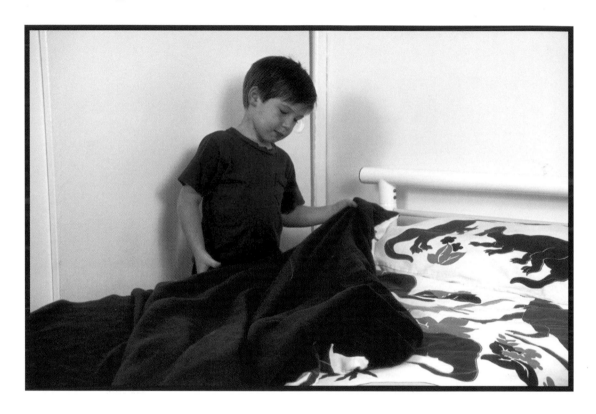

You can help with chores at home.

You can make your bed.

You can help set the table
for dinner.

You can give everyone a **napkin**.

How Can You Help in Your Neighborhood?

You can keep your neighborhood clean.

You can help rake leaves.

You can keep your
neighborhood pretty.

You can help plant a **garden**
with flowers.

How Do You Feel When You Help?

You can feel proud when you help others.

Helping others is a good thing to do.

You can make someone happy when you help.

It feels good when you can make someone else happy.

Quiz

How can you help?

Look for the answer on page 24.

Picture Glossary

cooperate
page 4

garden
page 19

napkin
page 17

23

Note to Parents and Teachers

Reading for information is an important part of a child's literacy development. Learning begins with a question about something. Help children think of themselves as investigators and researchers by encouraging their questions about the world around them. Each chapter in this book begins with a question. Read the question together. Look at the pictures. Talk about what you think the answer might be. Then read the text to find out if your predictions were correct. Think of other questions you could ask about the topic, and discuss where you might find the answers.

Index

bed. 16

chore. 16

cooperate 4

dinner 11, 17

dish 11

garden 19

job 5, 9, 13

napkin. 17

neighborhood. . . 7, 18–19

rake 18

Answer to quiz on page 22

You can put the trash into a trash can.

Kafka's Doubles

Utah Studies
in Literature and Linguistics

edited by

Gerhard P. Knapp — Luis Lorenzo-Rivero
Wolff A. von Schmidt

Vol. 15

Special Editor
Wolff A. von Schmidt

PETER LANG
Berne · Francfort/M. · Las Vegas

Kurt J. Fickert

Kafka's Doubles

PETER LANG
Berne · Francfort/M. · Las Vegas

CIP-Kurztitelaufnahme der Deutschen Bibliothek

Fickert, Kurt J.:
Kafka's doubles / Kurt J. Fickert. - Berne,
Francfort/M. [Frankfurt/M.], Las Vegas : Lang, 1979.
  (Utah studies in literature and linguistics ; Vol. 15)
  ISBN 3-261-03100-X

© Peter Lang Publishers Ltd., Berne (Switzerland) 1979
Successors of Herbert Lang & Co. Ltd., Berne

"We do not know, for Kafka did not know either."

(Heinz Politzer)

CONTENTS

		page
INTRODUCTION		9
CHAPTER I	: An Inner Biography	15
CHAPTER II	: Prague and Amerika	27
CHAPTER III	: At the Office and at the Bar of Justice	47
CHAPTER IV	: Castle and Burrow	67
CHAPTER V	: The Use and Abuse of the Double	81
CONCLUSIONS		89
BIBLIOGRAPHY		93
INDEX		99

INTRODUCTION

The field of Kafka studies establishes, once more, the validity of the French maxim that the more things change, the more they remain the same. Although critical literature concerning the Kafka canon has achieved the dimension of the colossal, the tenor of opinion has not become dramatically different: various interpretations of the symbolism (allegory may be discounted) in Kafka's work, made by various critics writing in the early years of his fame, have attained the stature of being authoritative without being definitive. Brod's and Tauber's basically religious reading of Kafka has not been refuted; rather, other points of view have been afforded an equal status, that of being "standard," even though divergent. The value of Politzer's esteemed explication, in which Kafka's conflict-ridden relationship to his father predominates, has not deteriorated. Less appreciated as a key work on Kafka, Neider's The Frozen Sea with its intensely Freudian hypotheses nevertheless maintains its position in the vanguard of the psychological or clinical attack on the Kafka "problem," as Flores' collection of essays terms the ambiguity inherent in Kafka. In the philosophical realm, Kafka's existential anguish, interpreted by Emrich and Sokel, is still the starting point for recent explorations of a literary continent, vast areas of which remain persistently dark.

Of the latest endeavors to let in the light, to clear up the obscurity which is the challenge Kafka found in life and reproduced in his work, most have both made inroads in the territory of the unknown and, paradoxically, have skirted the area. Thus Meno Spann's comprehensive, if not in-depth study of Kafka, published in 1976, has effectively emphasized the literary quality of Kafka's fiction, its falling into place in the tradition of European literature, while at the same time pronouncements are made which obfuscate what other critics have already made clear. Spann contends rather gratuitously, for instance, that "Kafka never concerned himself with the artist and his relation to society."[1] In like manner, Spann's contention that "Kafka's works do not express ideas but his feelings of insecurity and guilt [...] (op. cit., p. 178) beclouds the issue of Kafka's intent in writing which the principal thesis of the study has already defined. Relying equally on the work of earlier interpreters of Kafka, principally Politzer, Hillmann, Emrich, Walser, and Heinrich and Ingeborg Henel, Bert Nagel's Franz Kafka: Aspekte zur Interpretation und Wertung (1974) succeeds in maintaining

9

a level-headed approach to unraveling the Gordian knots in Kafka and contents itself with reiterating the themes overtly contained in the stories--the triad of guilt, judgment and punishment and an attempted explication of the inexplicable. But Nagel's occasional sorties upon hidden meanings are unproductive, e.g., his solution to the riddle of the execution machine which declares it to be simply the machine as the oppressor of humanity. Also appearing in 1974, Franz Kafka by Franz Kuna combines an insightful chapter on The Trial with a reading of The Castle which largely elaborates the theme of love as salvation evolved by Emrich.

Another recent book about Kafka by Ronald Gray, published in 1973, once again has as its principal feature a sane and non-contentious analysis of Kafka's work; in common with much of the latest Kafka criticism, it focuses on Kafka the writer, the literary artist. It avoids plunging into the abyss of obscurity: "The universal applicability some readers find was not put there by Kafka."[2] Another treatment of Kafka's intent as a writer, exhibiting, however, a greater degree of subtlety, is Anthony Thorlby's Kafka: A Study (1972); Thorlby finds that Kafka's fiction comments on itself as fiction and on Kafka as the writer of fiction. In essence, so Thorlby posits, Kafka is split into the intellect and the artist observing that intellect. While evolving this sophisticated thesis and making other provocative statements, Thorlby declines to give his book the aspect of the definitive and declares that it is impossible, and indeed unnecessary, to interpret all of the symbolism in Kafka.

The ongoing preoccupation of scholars with the Kafka canon has produced an equal number of books which deal with a specific area of his work. Its philosophical import is probed in Patrick Bridgwater's Kafka and Nietzsche (1974). Kafka the writer is again the central figure in the book, representing the Dionysian half of his personality, as Kafka the clerk does the Appollonian. While the relationship established by Bridgwater between Kafka's and Nietzsche's philosophies provides some new points of view, the contribution of the book to Kafka criticism consists largely of its setting forth additional interpretations of the stories which are worth considering; "Josephine, the Singer," for example, is construed as an illustration of Nietzschean amor fati: death is the highest form of life, silence is the highest form of art. Published in 1973, On Kafka's Castle by Richard Sheppard affords an additional vantage point from which to view that multifaceted structure; the book's supposition is that most of the elements in the novel serve as a mirror, externalizing K.'s inner conflicts. Also in 1973 Heinz Politzer edited a collection of essays about

Kafka's work: <u>Franz Kafka</u>; these are in the main reprints of the most important, that is, most effectively written short papers on the Kafka problem, among them the astute conclusions of Ingeborg Henel concerning "The Possibility of Interpreting Kafka" ("Die Deutbarkeit von Kafkas Werken"). She finds the key to interpreting Kafka in the proposition that, in encountering his fictitious world, Kafka encounters himself.

The present study proceeds in the direction which this and other recent Kafka criticism have taken. Predominant is the figure of Kafka the writer. That Kafka intended to create literature, a world of fiction, is a fact which finds its support in the nature of the works themselves, in the voluminous commentary he wrote in letters and diaries and in the very course his life took. There emerges from these elements, I have concluded, a pattern, both in the sense of a literary metaphor and in the sense of a <u>Lebensanschauung</u>, which must afford new insight in the Kafka canon. An explication of this motif of the double omnipresent in Kafka is my intent in writing this book. To explore this theme fully, I propose first to consider the events of Kafka's paradoxically uneventful life and to depict the evolution of a dichotomy in it which produced both the conflict-ridden man and the artist observing himself. Kafka's sense of mission as a writer, his conviction, shared by many German authors of the time, by Mann, Hesse and Musil, for instance, that the artist lives his life as a scapegoat for humanity, gave a <u>raison d'être</u> to the man Kafka and also provided the inner conflict which his works recreate.

Drawing on the literature which Kafka produced in roughly chronological order, together with pertinent autobiographical material from Kafka's journals and letters, I have tried to describe all facets of the motif of the <u>Doppelgänger</u> and/or double which a careful reading of the texts will display. I have related my interpretations of this material to relevant critical comment from a multitude of sources. The book ends with a summary of the results of this quest which, like Kafka's own, originates in the assumption that literature, the province of the written language, is the last refuge of meaning in life.

Introduction - Footnotes

[1] Meno Spann: Franz Kafka. Boston, Mass. 1976; p. 166.

[2] Ronald Gray: Franz Kafka. Cambridge, England, 1973; p. 125.

CHAPTER I

An Inner Biography

An account of Kafka's life can but be brief: his life was short and uneventful. In a perspicacious book of over 400 pages dealing with Kafka's work, Franz Kafka (Frankfurt am Main, 1960), Wilhelm Emrich provides anticlimactically, as an appendix, the necessary biographical information in five and a half pages. Norbert Fürst likewise leaves for the last in an imaginative study of Kafka's narratives, The Unlocked Hidden Doors of Franz Kafka (Die offenen Geheimtüren Franz Kafkas, Heidelberg, 1956), a one-paragraph summation of the essential facts of his life. Even when there is a detailed presentation of the circumstances under which Kafka lived at one particular time, as in Klaus Wagenbach's Franz Kafka: A Biography of His Youth (Franz Kafka: Eine Biographie seiner Jugend 1883-1912, Bern, 1958), half of the book consists of the documentation of trivialities. Paradoxically and appropriately, since, above all, Kafka's work is to be savored as paradox, the surface placidity of the course of his life fostered the exploration of an inner turmoil, to which he devoted himself and his literary endeavors. He once expressed his frustration at being unable to write an autobiography[1] but produced one nevertheless in a body of fiction, unrivaled in modern literature in both its subtlety and explicitness.

The antithetical element in Kafka's work, e.g., its validity as fiction in spite of its abuse of the principles of the art of fiction, appears initially in the factors which were responsible for his desire to be a writer. As the first child born (on July 3, 1883) to a successful, self-made business man, Herrmann Kafka, and his wife Julie (neé Löwy), Franz was ordained to follow in his father's footsteps. But there were counterforces which soon made themselves manifest, encouraging the development of the introversion and self-indulgence of the artist. In his mother's family the men were intellectual and individualistic. Physically, Franz came to resemble the Löwy side of the family, growing tall and gaunt, lacking the substantial girth of his father, to which, in contrast, he related his increasing sense of inadequacy. The fact that he eventually had three sisters, to whom he was bound by an awareness of his responsibility toward them as an older brother, made his self-proclaimed deficiencies more pronounced. In addition, his ambivalent feelings toward his mother, who subjugated herself completely to her husband and all but abandoned her family in order to work in his establishment, acerbated Kafka's sense of isolation and failure.

In the meantime the milieu in which Kafka lived afforded his inner conflicts further substantiality. His was a German enclave in the Czech city of Prague; as a member of this minority he was doubly estranged because of his Jewish faith. Even within the Jewish community, however, he was not secure. Under his father's tutelage he came, in the manner of the "Western" contingent of the Jewish nation, to suspect Jewish orthodoxy, while he waxed enthusiastic about the sectarianism of a group of Jewish actors who had taken their East-European heritage on tour, in the form of drama and song. To crown the complexity of these relationships, Kafka had a German schooling.

School, culminating in graduation from the German university of Prague, represented to Kafka both the shackles of conformity, enslavement to the middle-class values for which his father stood, and the opportunity for the unfettered pursuit of antibourgeois aestheticism, in partnership with new-found friends. As a student Kafka was equally successful in maintaining an appearance of being well integrated in the educational system and in establishing himself as a member of a literary circle with its (in this case literally) Bohemian atmosphere. The beginning of his schooling instituted, nevertheless, his excursion into the realm of Angst, physical and mental trepidation, in which he spent the rest of his life. Almost every day, as his governess accompanied him to the schoolgrounds, she would, as a whim perhaps, warn him of some punishment which would be meted out to him as a consequence of his willfulness.

His first attempts at writing stories similarly established a pattern. His Journals[2] recount the unfortunate results of his exhibiting an early endeavor in the field of the novel. Furnishing a prototype, the plot involved two brothers who represent opposing forces, the one an emigrant to America, the other a prisoner in Europe (cf. Bendemann and his friend in Russia in "The Judgment"--"Das Urteil"). Proud of his inventiveness, Kafka took advantage of the occasion, the visit of relatives, and passed a manuscript page on to his uncle to read. This first reader of Kafka glanced over the text and, having remarked casually to the gathering, as if to no one in particular, "The usual stuff," handed it back. The embarrassment which this disinterestedness effected could well have been the source of Kafka's often expressed need to discredit

16

his work and of his just as often expressed need to set for himself, as an author, the highest of standards. The seriousness with which he regarded his fledgling literary pursuits, undertaken, no doubt, in imitation of and in competition with his peers at school who were intellectually gifted, exhibited itself in the few close friendships with them he was able to establish. His first affections he reserved for Oskar Pollak, a fellow-student at the <u>Gymnasium</u>, and his letters to Pollak, concerned with maintaining their friendship, not only dealt with but also became a literary link between them. To Pollak, as a sign of his loyalty, Kafka sent his early work. The tensions, in the midst of which Kafka's writing evolved, particularly those which already existed between Kafka and his father, emerge in vivid fashion in one of the letters; here Kafka cries out: "God doesn't want me to write, but I, I have to."[3] In another letter to Pollak the intensity of Kafka's preoccupation with literature makes itself felt: "Many a book," he wrote (<u>Letters</u>, p. 20), "serves as a key to the unknown rooms in one's own castle." Kafka failed in his first attempt to live both in the world of the imagination and in the real world, in which Pollak's friendship gave him a vantage point ("You were, besides much else, something like a window for me," he confided to Pollak, <u>Letters, ibid.</u>), for, lacking the patience to try to understand the complexity of Kafka's personality and also, perhaps, a capacity to comprehend the potentialities of Kafka's talent, Pollak let their youthful friendship take its natural course, from neglect to oblivion. About a decade later, Pollak died in the First World War.

In place of the flawed relationship with Pollak, Kafka soon forged a bond of friendship with Max Brod, a fellow-student at the university and a prominent member of the group of intellectuals to whom Kafka was drawn because his interests and social background coincided with theirs. Brod more than compensated for the inadequacies of Pollak; he recognized, almost intuitively, a genius in Kafka which surpassed his own considerable abilities. Accordingly he encouraged Kafka in his writing and fostered its publication. Not only did he eventually prevent the destruction of the major portion of Kafka's work, more importantly for Kafka himself, he persevered in his efforts to lure his dubious friend into a commitment to being an author. In addition, Brod fortified Kafka in his efforts to deal with his oppressive situation at home. Encouraging Kafka to free himself, at least temporarily, from his family ties by taking him along on vacation trips, he established a route of escape, which Kafka was then able to pursue on his own. On

17

an early occasion Brod proposed that they keep a travel journal together, which evolved into a co-authored novel <u>Richard</u> <u>und</u> <u>Samuel</u>, a
project later abandoned by mutual consent.

All the while Kafka was readying himself for a role in the bureaucratic
world. After a few tentative steps in the direction of studying literature,
Kafka set out on a successful university career in law. Having obtained
a degree in 1906, he followed the course prescribed for beginning law-
yers--a year's unremunerated service in the law courts, an unrewarding
and exhausting start in business (with an insurance firm, the Assicura-
zioni Generali) and finally placement which held promise. Offered em-
ployment in 1908 at the <u>Arbeiter</u>-<u>Unfall</u>-<u>Versicherungs</u>-<u>Anstalt</u>, a quasi-
governmental institution which processed the claims of injured workers,
Kafka accepted with alacrity because he was afforded working hours
compatible with the kind of regimen he wanted to keep--morning and
early afternoon at the office, rest in the late afternoon, writing until
past midnight and little sleep. His association with the <u>Anstalt</u> seemed
satisfactory and lasted; Kafka never revealed to the staff the mental
anguish which he underwent when engaged in any activity but writing.
His physical decline, due to tuberculosis, produced requests for sick-
leaves and eventually for a pension, which was granted in 1922, two
years before his death.

But the efficient and circumspect young man who worked in the govern-
ment offices was leading a double life. Every free moment he devoted
to his development as a writer. His earliest literary experiments, including the fragment of the novel about two brothers who contend with
one another and a second novel, to whose dichotomous title Kafka later
referred--<u>The</u> <u>Child</u> <u>and</u> <u>the</u> <u>City</u> (<u>Das</u> <u>Kind</u> <u>und</u> <u>die</u> <u>Stadt</u>), are lost.
Undoubtedly, Kafka did not know when his desire to be a writer first
made itself manifest--when had it not been there? Its obsessive nature
became gradually apparent, even though he all but avoided publication
of his work. He seemed unable to distinguish it from the journals and
diaries he kept, initially at the instigation of Max Brod. Also upon the
insistence of Brod, he allowed two short pieces, descriptive sketches,
to appear in the magazine <u>Hyperion</u> in 1909.

Another aspect of his situation, which assumed the proportions of a
catastrophe for Kafka, was the conflict between his writing and his per-
forming conscientiously his tasks at the office. After several years of
work at the <u>Arbeiter</u>-<u>Unfall</u>-<u>Versicherungs</u>-<u>Anstalt</u>, he had already
come to the conclusion and stated as a principle in his <u>Journals</u>

(p. 57 f.) that he was torn apart by his two vocations: "Now these two vocations (Berufe) can never reach an accord and achieve a common happiness. The least bit of happiness in the one becomes a great unhappiness in the other [...]. At the office I fulfill my obligations outwardly, but not my inner obligations, and every unfulfilled inner obligation becomes a disaster (Unglück), which I cannot shake off." At the root of the conviction that he was involved in a continuous contest between warring selves lay Kafka's new-found faith in his calling as a writer, leading to his firm resolve that nothing else could or should matter. A subsequent diary entry, in 1912, poses his predicament: "When it had become clear in my physical self (Organismus) that writing was the most rewarding disposition in my nature, everything concentrated itself around [this tendency] and depleted all [my] capacities which pertained to the pleasures of sex, of eating and drinking, of philosophic ruminations and, most especially, of [enjoying] music" (Journals, p. 129). Under these circumstances he allowed himself to be persuaded by a publisher, whom Brod had alerted to Kafka's talent, to put together for appearance in book form a parsimonious amount of the sketches he had produced in his journals. He also began the ambitious project of writing a novel; it was to be One Who Vanished (Der Verschollene or, by Brod's emendation, Amerika).

With the proof sheets of his collection of prose studies, published later that year, 1912, by Rowohlt with the title of Observation (Betrachtung),4 Kafka appeared at Brod's home one evening, and a series of events began which determined, as if by decree of some high court, the destiny of Kafka the writer and Kafka the young man with obligations to his family and his employers. He was introduced to Felice Bauer, a young woman from Berlin, stopping over in Prague and visiting the Brod family briefly. She was neither particularly attractive nor brilliant, but at this fateful moment, with his first book in his hands, Kafka once more turned life into literature and fixed upon Felice Bauer as an appropriate symbol. She would be the sign of his ultimate triumph, the angel who would lead him to the promised land in which the writer lived in harmony with the bourgeois world. Their acquaintanceship was at first basically literary: having spent but a few hours with her, he posted letter after letter to her in Berlin, for a considerable time, one letter a day. This courtship by mail concerned itself with his particular quandary, how to be a writer and at the same time a breadwinner, the head of a household. Unwilling to play only the passive role of correspondent, Felice eventually prevailed upon Kafka to come to Berlin. The results of his first visit were rather inconclusive, but the promise of a proper engagement became faintly audible in the correspondence which continued unabated. Kafka travelled a second time to Berlin, and on June 1, 1914, Kafka and Felice Bauer were engaged.

This surrender to the requirements of middle-class society was the price Kafka paid for a period of creative activity following his encounter with Felice. Soon after their first meeting he had written "The Judgment" ("Das Urteil"). This burst of creativity which lasted one night represented for him a moment of fulfillment as a writer. He felt that he had reached the pinnacle of achievement, a height he was never able, in his own mind, to reach again. Further accomplishments in writing, among them the completion of "Metamorphosis" ("Die Verwandlung"), produced an intensification of the inner conflict between the writer and the bourgeois.

A note of desperation soon became dominant in his letters to Felice: "For my writing I require [a kind of] seclusion other than that of the hermit--that would not be enough: I require the seclusion of a dead man."[5] He did not conceal from her the fact that literature demanded of him the exclusion of all social intercourse: "I abhor everything which does not involve literature; it bores me to make conversation, even when it concerns literature [...]" (to Felice Bauer, July 21, 1913). His journals repeat this theme (p. 311) and reveal, as indeed his fiction does, the almost pathological abhorrence with which Kafka the writer regarded the situation of Kafka the engaged young lawyer: "Coitus," he confided to himself (p. 315), "[is to be considered] as the punishment for being together." In a subsequent entry (p. 316), he posed suicide, a leap from the window, as the solution to his dilemma. At times the division in him even took on a physical aspect; the journals record this confrontation: "A while ago I looked at myself carefully in the mirror [...]. The look in my eyes is not at all decadent; there is not a trace [of decadence]. Nor is the look in my eyes child-like, rather, unexpectedly, energetic, but perhaps it was only observant, since I was [indeed] observing myself and wanted to frighten myself" (p. 342). In describing this process of self-appraisal Kafka not only provided a clue to his intent in writing but also characterized the tenor of all his work.

Kafka's troubled relationship with Felice Bauer lasted for several years; for a time it even involved him in an acquaintanceship and correspondence which duplicated the problematical one with Felice--the recipient of his attention was Felice's friend Grete Bloch.[6] Grete was involved

in the dissolution of her friends' engagement, as a sympathetic by-
stander. Later, after the resumption of letter-writing and several con-
ciliatory meetings, Kafka and Felice were once again engaged. The
inevitable break which occurred once more proved to be permanent,
since Kafka had discovered an irrefutable argument against marriage--
his illness.

The conflict which Kafka's friendship with Felice, together with his
two vocations, engendered, was the foundation on which the rising
structure of his fiction rested. In his writing Kafka strove for new
achievement; he considered his early work, "The Judgment" in particular, to be lyrical, rather than epic (cf. Letters, p. 149). These
sketches are self-portraits in prose, and their medium is the metaphor. Already in "Metamorphosis," which followed "The Judgment,"
however, the symbol has supplanted the simile as the main factor in
the story, for, as Kafka's commitment to writing grew, the epic
quality in his work increased. The deliberate and controlled fashion-
ing of a fictitious world, rife with symbolism, prevails in the stories
which Kafka wrote in the period between "In the Penal Colony" ("In
der Strafkolonie") and the Country Doctor collection (Ein Landarzt).
Subsequent to the diagnosis of tuberculosis, which was, for Kafka,
both a death sentence and a sentencing to exile in the world of the
writer, a third phase of his work evolved. It combined the extreme
introversion of the early pieces with the element of an inner conflict genuinely externalized which characterizes the fiction of the in-
tervening years. The complete Dichter, Kafka ultimately concerned
himself with depicting human fate in the guise of his own, the writer's. In a letter written in 1922 he devised a "definition" of the function of the writer: "[The writer--Schriftsteller] is the scapegoat for
humanity; he allows man to delight in sin without a sense of guilt, or
almost without a sense of guilt" (Letters, p. 386).

But Kafka's resolve to be a writer was not unwavering. For periods
he resumed work at the Anstalt. In 1919, for a briefer time, he was
engaged again (to Julie Wohryzek). In writing a voluminous letter to
his father ("Brief an den Vater"), he sought to eradicate the conflict
in the relationship which had, in part, generated his need to write.
These efforts not to lose contact with the real world reached their
climax in Kafka's affair with Milena Jesenska,[7] married and Christian, with whom he became acquainted, as the Czech translator of
his stories, by correspondence. The similarities between Kafka's
relationship with Milena and with Felice are striking. Both women

sought to draw Kafka out of a literary and into a personal acquaintanceship. Kafka was his usual reticent self; "Love means," he informed
Milena, "that you are the knife with which I explore myself."[8] The
symbol of the double served, in Kafka's explication of their relationship, to make clear to Milena that she was in love with a phantom,
someone who was only the words she was reading. "You forget, Milena," he told her, "that we are only standing next to one another,
observing this being before us which I am; but I as the onlooker am,
first and foremost, insubstantial."[9] Thus Kafka foreordained the end
of the affair; there were several partings and then a last one.

Even more important than these events in Kafka's constant transliteration of life into literature was the deterioration of his health, the
result of his "wound," the symbol he had intuively devised for his incapacity to lead a "normal" life (cf. Letters, p. 160). Now he concluded
that his intellect, his will to be a writer, had triumphed over his natural self. His journals (p. 544) describe the effect of the accord
reached by the material and immaterial Kafkas: "The systematic destruction of my self in the course of the years is astounding [...]. The
intellect (Geist), which has brought this about, must now be celebrat-
ing its success." But this forced resolution of his conflicts Kafka accepted as a literary challenge. The writer whose goal had been self-
expression, "the representation of my dream-like inner life" (Journals,
p. 420), was overshadowed by the artist with an ideal--the author "who
can transport the world to the realm of the inviolable, the true, the
immutable" (Journals, p. 534).

Kafka now became the invisible observer of the invisible Dichter-figure.
"Begin to see," he commanded himself (Journals, p. 511), "who you
are, instead of calculating what is to become of you." In the pose of
philosopher and seer he considered the stance of the writer: "I would
be content to be standing directly next to myself; I would be content to
be able to conceive of the place on which I am standing as being another
place" (loc. cit. , p. 561). In his notebooks this ultimate stage in producing fiction is depicted: "Writing denies itself to me. Therefore [this]
plan for autobiographical investigations. Not biography, but investigation and location of the most infinitesimal components. Out of these I
intend to build myself up afterwards, like someone who wants to construct next to his house, which is deteriorating, a substantial one, if
possible out of the material of the old."[10]

Paradoxically, life afforded this self-absorbed Dichter, after he had shut out the world, some of the comforts of the world. He became aware of an intimation of the recognition which he was to receive as a writer. [11] A relationship with a young woman Dora Diamant (Dymant) proved satisfactory, and the friendship of a young medical student, Robert Klopstock, gave him the sense of having progeny. These triumphs were insignificant, however, in the light of the triumph of his "wound," physically tuberculosis, figuratively the writer's death-wish; on June 3, 1924, Kafka died in Kierling. [12]

A final conflict in Kafka's life expressed itself in his instructions to Max Brod to burn his manuscripts after his death. To an extent, he passed judgment with this decree on the act of his having committed himself to writing. In a letter to Brod, dated August 5, 1922, Kafka had already voiced his despair at his having shunned the "normal" life; writing, he held, was serving the devil--"this descent to the forces of darkness, this unleashing of demons held in check by nature, of dubious passions (Umarmungen) and what all else may occur down below, about which one remains ignorant, when one is writing stories up above in the sunlight."

Despite the hopelessness of the writer's situation, the incommensurability of the written word with reality in its most potent form--death, Kafka accepted the inevitability of the choice he had made, the wound he had incurred, as he assured Robert Klopstock: "This writing is for me [...] the most important thing on earth, like psychosis to a psychotic [...] or like pregnancy to a [pregnant] woman" (Letters, p. 431). But behind the ideal figure of the Dichter, into which Kafka had tried to transform himself, there remained, perhaps only as substantial as a shadow, the other Kafka, the son of Herrmann Kafka, the lawyer, the suitor of Felice Bauer and Milena Jesenska. It was he who had given the "letter to his father" not to his father, but to his mother, who, as its author might have anticipated, returned it undelivered. It was he who left notebooks and manuscripts in Milena's care, removed from the threat of an auto-da-fé. And it was surely he who commissioned the lone champion of the genius of Franz Kafka to contemplate the obliteration of his three unfinished novels, the countless fragments of stories, the journals, and, by and large, all his life and work. To the very end this dualism in Kafka persisted, and Brod understood the situation so that he could, by listening to the one voice, which cried out against waste, save the other, which informed mankind.

Chapter I - Footnotes

[1] "I would alleviate my longing to write an autobiography at the very moment which set me free from [my work at] the office," Franz Kafka; Tagebücher 1910-1923. N.p. 1954; p. 194. My translation, here and elsewhere from the German, unless otherwise indicated.

[2] Tagebücher, p. 39 f. Further references to the Tagebücher are given in the text under the rubric Journals.

[3] Franz Kafka: Briefe 1902-1924. New York, 1958; p. 21. References to this book appear hereafter in the text as Letters.

[4] The title given the translation of these sketches into English, Meditation, seems to me to be unfortunately imprecise, since Betrachtung has the connotation of notetaking and refers to the written word.

[5] Franz Kafka in: Erich Heller & Joachim Beug (ed.): Dichter über ihre Dichtungen. München 1969; p. 135. To Felice Bauer, Prague, June 16, 1913.

[6] See Elias Canetti: Der andere Prozess. München 1969. He proposes that Kafka, now committed to marry Felice, turned his attention to Grete Bloch, writing to her, who was out of his reach as his fiancée's best friend, the kind of courtship letter he had previously written to Felice.

[7] Kafka confided to Max Brod (Letters, p. 317) that he was attracted sexually to girls who were out of his reach and that he considered sexuality a kind of threat. There followed this confession: "As long as she [any woman] withheld herself from me (F) or as long as we were together (M), it was only a threat from afar, and not even considerably afar; as soon as some slight thing happened, however everything went to pieces." Kafka's "(F)" and "(M)" are readily decipherable.

[8] Franz Kafka: Briefe an Milena. New York 1952; p. 225.

[9] Briefe an Milena. P. 238.

[10] Franz Kafka: Hochzeitsvorbereitungen auf dem Lande. New York, 1953; p. 388.

[11] In 1915 Kafka was awarded the Fontane prize for literary achievement on the recommendation of Carl Sternheim, who, having declined it, was persuaded to pass it on. Although a number of prominent writers took occasion to declare their admiration for Kafka's work, he remained, on the whole, unrecognized during his lifetime.

12 See Letters, p. 385. Kafka writes: "Reasons for fearing death can be divided into two main categories. First, [the writer] is terribly afraid to die because he has never lived [...]. The second reason [...] is [this] train of thought: 'What I have pretended (gespielt) will really happen. All my life I have died, and now I will die for real [...]. I haven't bought off [death] by writing.'"

CHAPTER II

Prague and Amerika

Among the earliest of Kafka's prose pieces still extant is "Description of a Struggle" ("Beschreibung eines Kampfes"), two sections of which introduce the Stories and Prose Sketches (Erzählungen und kleine Prosa), constituting the collected works' first volume. [1] Appropriately, the title of the initial story emphasizes the descriptive element in its structure and the theme, which concerns a contest; all of Kafka's subsequent work has these two characteristics. The nature of the opposing forces cannot, however, be easily ascertained, neither here, in these exercises in expressionistic prose written by a covert author, nor later, in the prose masterpieces of Kafka, the deliberate artist. In the first of the two excerpts, "Conversation with the Supplicant" ("Gespräch mit dem Beter"), for instance, the protagonist, the "I," has no identity except for his compulsive concern for the supplicant. In turn, this stranger, whose bizarre behavior fascinates the writer-observer, seems to exist only as a challenge to the mind of the other man, familiar with a world in which everything, including words, behaves rationally. A comparison with the situation in "In the Penal Colony," one of Kafka's defter stories, seems inescapable, since there, too, a "scientist" is confronted by both a mystical machine and its fanatical proponent. Since the relationship between the two men in both instances consists solely of the mutuality of their interests, the conclusion must be drawn that they are two aspects of one person and that the conversations, which, peculiarly, serve the function of describing the association between the characters, are a monologue, Kafka talking to himself. The supposition arises that, in the earlier story, the narrator is, in the main, identical with Franz Kafka, the aspiring author and incipient lawyer. Opposite him ("gegenüber" is one of Kafka's favorite words, often in the guise of prefix, noun and gerundive), there is a nebulous image, a form in a faded mirror. "There has never been a time," the supplicant says, "in which I was convinced, through the agency of my self, of my existence."[2] This other self has the insubstantiality of an ideal, particularly of a literary ideal: the realization, through writing, of the abstraction which is the entire self. Thus there is, in effect, a twofold doubling; the breakdown of the immaterial Kafka, a mental projection, into the fictitious "I" and his alter ego, the supplicant, and the breakdown of the actual Kafka into the rational observer and the supra-rational writer and instigator of the schism. In

dealing with the question of how Kafka's work can be interpreted, Ingeborg C. Henel makes the significant comment that "the reader sees
everything divided not once, but twice."[3] Even here, at the beginning,
Kafka's work exhibits its chief characteristic, the manysidedness of its
point of view, the source of its appeal because it represents "the possibility of finding an internal way of grasping the meaning of meaning
(which in Kafka's case meant the meaning of writing, the meaning of
words)."[4]

The second of the "Description of a Struggle" fragments, "Conversation with a Drunken Man," proceeds with the quest for a sense of reality, for self-assurance. The opening "dialogue," in actuality an interior monologue, in which the ego and alter ego speak alternately, takes
up the theme of the transliteration of the insubstantial world into the
tangibility (later Kafka will call it truth) of a concept, a structure of
words; for instance, Kafka proposes that the Virgin Mary column in
the square will lose its ominous quality when he calls it "moon cast-
ing a yellow light." This phantasy-making or conceptualizing part
of his inner self the protagonist labels a drunken man; the "plot" of
the story consists of an encounter with the externalized double of the
inebriate self, whose existence, however, depends on the creative
will, the naming ability, of the physically present "I," the narrator.
In the end, the two, amanuensis and drunken man, link arms, supporting one another, cloaking one another in the costume of reality
(clothes are a ubiquitous symbol in the Kafka canon).

These first "descriptive" pieces are word-games, employing metaphor in place of characterization and in place of style: "The wind on
the square is excited. The tip of the town-hall tower describes little
circles [...]. All the windowpanes make noise, and the lamp-posts
bend over like bamboo" (Stories, p. 19). In his next substantial literary exercise, written in 1907 and, prototypally, left unfinished, "Wedding Preparations in the Country" ("Hochzeitsvorbereitungen auf dem
Lande"), Kafka has already begun to attempt to create a fictitious and,
therefore, real world, one removed from an arrangement of random
musings. The title suggests the functioning of a plot, still only vaguely
present, and the protagonist has a name, Eduard Raban, the first of
many disguises for "Kafka": it has the same number of letters, the
same vowels, and is similar to "raven" ("Rabe"), appropriately a
member of the family of blackbirds, crows, the meaning of "Kafka"
in Czech (cf. "The Hunter Gracchus," a translation into Latin; perhaps Karl Rossmann's identification of himself in Amerika as "negro,"

"Neger"). In the course of presenting the theme of the story, the dual nature of Eduard Raban, Kafka introduces his most famous metaphor: "I have, while I lie in bed, the form of a great beetle [...]."[5] Raban keeps this "ideal" self, because it fulfills his longing for seclusion, hidden in his room while his persona, the self which confronts society, undertakes the journey to his bride. Marriage as a symbol for social interaction, for the bourgeois world, in which conformity and success are the principal values, makes its initial appearance in "Wedding Preparations in the Country" and then becomes commonplace in Kafka's work. Also typical is the story's development by means of chance encounters between the protagonist and a series of friends and strangers. These "companions," "Begleiter," as Martin Walser names them, serve, according to him, to distract the hero from paying attention to himself, from reaching his goal.[6] Raban does not find his way to the place in the country where the wedding preparations are underway, not only because the story has no ending but also because Raban is one of the many (if not all) protagonists in Kafka who travel only in the labyrinth of the mind, with its endless network of misleading rationalizations.

Since a good deal of the material in Observation (Betrachtung, published in 1913) appears to have been written before "Wedding Preparations in the Country," the lack of structure in these prose pieces, some of which are short and metaphoric enough to be poems, suggests l'art pour l'art or the artist as Sunday painter; nevertheless, Kafka's insight into the paradoxical nature of existence is already deep. The few sentences which constitute "The Trees" ("Die Bäume"), for instance, foreshadow in their perspicacity the later "Of Metaphors" ("Von den Gleichnissen," 1922): "For we are like tree-trunks in the snow. Apparently they stand unsupported, and with a little push one should be able to topple them. No, one can't do that, for they are fixed firmly in the ground. But, consider this, even that is only apparently so" (Stories, p. 44). In these brief lines the intent of all of Kafka's fiction becomes clear: Kafka wants to create a crisis for the mind. As Helmut Kuhn has pointed out in his book on existentialism, "the word crisis is derived from a Greek verb which means to separate (as with a sieve), to choose, to test, or to judge [...]."[7] In Kafka, however, the resolution of the crisis does not and cannot occur, since, all being relative, there are no valid criteria against which the conflicting contentions can be critically examined; lacking commitment, Kafka ponders the existentialist dilemma and takes flight from it--therefore, in addition, his stories present an unending series of comings and goings.

In some of the stories in the collection Observation which were written five or six years later than "The Trees," Kafka explores themes which will become central in his work. The symbol of the bachelor for the outsider-artist begins its evolution in the half-page narrative entitled "The Bachelor's Misfortunes" ("Das Unglück des Jungesellen"), written in November, 1911. The misery which Kafka imagines will be his lot if he should remain unmarried has as its source his observation of his uncle, Rudolf Löwy. His letters reveal that Uncle Rudolf, whom Kafka liked but did not admire, presented an image which served as a projection of how Kafka saw himself in the future. Initially, the figure of his uncle fulfilled the purpose of Kafka's father by providing a bad example. "In former times," Kafka explained to his friend Robert Klopstock, "my father used to say, when I had done something stupid, which was in reality only the consequence of some basic flaw in me: 'Just like Rudolf!' [...]. The painful repetition of the comparison, the almost physical difficulty in avoiding, at all cost, a path, which one had previously not even conceived of, and finally my father's abilitiy to be convincing or, if you will, his malediction, had the effect of my coming at least to resemble my uncle" (Letters, p. 361). Eventually, Rudolf Löwy's ineffectual existence as a bachelor was for Kafka the equivalent of the unlived life of the writer. The journals' comment on the situation has the usual paradoxical turn of phrase: "Down to the details [Uncle Rudolf] was a charicature of me; essentially, however, I am a charicature of him" (p. 559). In his bachelor uncle the young Kafka saw an externalized version of the Doppelgänger who was beginning to take shape in his mind and in his stories.

Another symbol which appears as but a brief entry in Observation and of which Kafka was later to make extensive use is that of clothing. In the sketch "Clothes," not even a page long, Kafka poses a dichotomy: clothes versus character or identity. In observing the clothes that people wear, Kafka comes to the conclusion that through constant use apparel must become heavy, dusty and shabby. People who never change clothes will make themselves laughable, he proposes. The metaphoric language in the "story" indicates that the opposite of this adherence to a routine, this conforming to a set pattern, which may originally even have had some validity, is the liberation of the self, the exercise of the self's right and need to develop. Kafka restates this principle by depicting beauty in young women as an external factor which fades and destroys itself when it, presumably, takes the place of inner growth, the blossoming of the self. It is the basic image of clothing, however, which Kafka retains for further elaboration in his work. Its final and climactic occurrence occupies the closing pages of The Castle; here the landlady of the Inn of the Masters (Herrenhof) acknowledges that K. comprehends the significance of clothes and, perhaps as a gesture of reconciliation, offers to invite him to view the new dresses she expects to arrive for her. Kafka's unusual preoccupation with clothes is practically the sole "abnormal" feature in his dreaming, according to an analysis of the content of his dreams undertaken by Hall and Lind; this study of Franz Kafka which proceeds by comparing the material in his dreams with that of a group of young men of the same age offers as a collatoral conclusion about the personality revealed in his dreaming the thesis that Kafka did not merely transcribe dreams but produced his work as the deliberate and consumate artist who was very much aware of the potency of the subconscious mind.

Also giving clear evidence of the direction which Kafka's fiction was to take and, in addition, providing a foretaste of the style which Kafka developed so individually is the brief "The Wish to be an Indian" ("Wunsch, Indianer zu werden"); it consists of one sentence, introduced by two clauses in the subjunctive, followed by a series of main clauses in the indicative (cf. "Up in the Gallery" -- "Auf der Galerie"). But the story begins with the title, which Kafka never affixes casually. It establishes that the theme of the sketch is the desire for a transformation. The words of the text themselves accomplish this acquisition of a new personality by making the unreal real, by passing from the mood of the possible to the mood of the factual. At the same time, that which is physically present, the horse and the field, together with the rider, becomes transcendent. This prose, poised on the border between the concrete and the invisible, seems almost to have evolved from Novalis's concept of magic idealism, which proposes generation and regeneration as the means for an exchange between the realms of reality and imagination. Involved is the principle pertaining to creative writing which the poet Marianne Moore employs in arriving at her definition of "Poetry": "imaginary gardens with real toads in them."

Much more an actual "story" and almost a bridge between the early prose fragments and Kafka's first accomplished work of fiction "The Judgment," the last selection in Observation, "The State of Misery" ("Unglücklichsein"), depicts two kinds of conflict and presents a problem to which there is no solution. Another instance of the juxtaposition of the material and the immaterial occurs first. A ghost appears to the story's protagonist; although the apparition has the form of a child, the narrator addresses the nocturnal visitor in his room with "Sie," which German reserves as a term of respect. (The forms of address which Kafka applies vary from normal usage to such an extent that they require a separate study.) The conversation between the ghost and the young man in "The State of Misery" establishes the relationship between them, namely, the identity they share. After a debate on the question of whether the apparition is forcing his presence on the narrator or whether the narrator has, instead, imprisoned the child in his room, the protagonist makes this rebuttal: "You say your nature compels you to talk to me in this way [...]. That's very good of your nature. Your nature is my nature, and if I maintain a friendly relationship with you because of my nature, then you can but do the same" (Stories, p. 47). The young man and the child are obviously different aspects of the same individual, Franz Kafka. Because he is indeed a ghost and moreover a child, this facet of Kafka's self has an association with the imagination, with the phantasy-making which is a part of childhood. In this respect, the child represents the writer. His other or opposing self is the "real" young man who has a room in which he sits and writes or which he leaves in the course of his "normal" activities. The conflict implicit in the situation involves justifying the existence of either one of the personalities at the expense of the other. There is no resolution because the young man gives up the struggle temporarily, puts on his hat and coat and goes out. Using a device, typical in his fiction, the intrusion of realistic detail, Kafka closes his ghost story on this note: "And I went to the night-stand, where I lighted the candle. At that time I had neither gas nor electric light in my room" (Stories, p. 47).

In this realm of the everday world the second part of the story begins. On the stairs, significant as a place of rising and descending, the young man encounters a fellow-boarder. Although he is also addressed with "Sie," the polite form of the pronoun "you," the intimacy of the relationship between the man on the stairs and the young man is immediately clear: "So, you're on your way out again, are you, you good-for-nothing (Lump)," the boarder comments. The tone is that of Kafka's father, as Kafka has reproduced it countless times in letters, journals and stories. The El-Greco-like distortion in depicting the figure of the boarder, foreshadowing the portraiture of the father in "The Judgment," further identifies the person whom Kafka confronts as he leaves his room: he is immense in comparison to the story's protagonist; as he pauses on the stairway his one leg is two steps above the other, and during the conversation he climbs higher and higher so that his closing remark is hurled from far above, echoing down the stairwell. The discussion between the man descending and the man ascending concerns itself with the problem of the ghost (visually there is a suggestion of the scene in "Before the Law"--"Vor dem Gesetz," in which the gatekeeper begins to tower more and more over the diminishing form of the man from the country). The boarder, or the father, treats the entire matter as a joke and duplicates the attitude of Kafka's father toward his writing. Playfully, the boarder volunteers to deal with the ghost in his own fashion, much as in "The Judgment" Mr. Bendemann claims at first not to believe in Georg's friend in Russia and then claims to have won him over. The conclusion of "The State of Misery" lacks the definitiveness with which "The Judgment" closes; here the protagonist retreats to his room after having made a plaintive plea that he be allowed to keep to himself his ghost, his private self-- the writer. The young man's last words to the malicious boarder are a threat: "If you take away my ghost from me up there [in my room], then we will be on the outs, for good" (Stories, p. 49).

Bringing the proof sheets of "The State of Misery" and the other pieces in Observation to Max Brod as a sign of his first success as a writer, Kafka unexpectedly met Felice Bauer in Brod's home and soon thereafter produced, as the result of the fervor of a single night's writing, "The Judgment" ("Das Urteil"). It is dedicated to Felice and records the change which had taken place in his life as a consequence of their acquaintanceship, at this point through correspondence. Very similar in its structure to "The State of Misery," "The Judgment" begins with a confrontation between a young man and a ghostly friend--his existence in the flesh is problematical. In writing "The Judgment," Kafka developed his skills in the art of creating fiction to such a high degree that he himself approved of the work and heralded its finesse. Two of his accomplishments are the unfolding of a story and the establishing of separate identities for three people, although there is no plot, only the inner development of the protagonist, who is, in fact, the sole character in "The Judgment." He is Georg Bendemann. In his Journals (p. 297) Kafka elaborately explains the pseudonym which Bendemann represents: the "mann" is extraneous; the "Bende" has the same number of letters as "Kafka," with the vowels occurring in the same position. Kafka begins his story by presenting a symbolic act: Bendemann is writing, and it later becomes clear that he has been writing in secret for some time, sending letters to a friend living in obscurity in Russia. At the end of the current letter he makes a reluctant confession: he has become engaged to Frieda Brandenfeld. In choosing this name for the fictitious fiancée Kafka has explained (Journals, p. 297) that he intended a reference to Felice, since her name has the same number of letters, and to the province of Brandenburg, where she lived, as well as an association between "field" and the occupation which her last name indicates: "Bauer," "farmer."

Georg[8] has qualms about revealing his successes in the social and business world to his friend because these triumphs must stand in contrast to the defeats with which his friend has met in Russia (he has also grown sick). The antithetical nature of the relationship between the two characters is obvious, and, furthermore, points to the mutuality of their concerns. That Kafka is portraying himself and his Doppelgänger is the consensus of critical opinion, e.g., "[Bendemann's friend in Petersburg] is none other than Georg Bendemann's (alias Franz Kafka's) other self."[9] The nature of this alter ego is that of the outsider, an intruder in the "normal" world like the child-ghost in "The State of Misery" (cf. also the title One Who Vanished). The symbol of the recluse, engaged in some hidden and meaningless activity, lends itself to interpretation as that of the writer. In the correspondence between Georg and his friend in Russia Kafka depicts both the link between the two and the source of their contending with one another. The protagonist in "The Judgment" wants, on the one hand, to maintain the life-line of writing which supports his ephemeral   self, and, on the other hand, to break off the relationship which threatens the well-being of the material self.

At this point, with the struggle between his two selves left undecided, Georg Bendemann, like the protagonist in "The State of Misery," has a confrontation with a father-figure, here his actual father, the elder Bendemann. With the appearance of this character another occasion of doubling has taken place, since Georg Bendemann's father is also Herrmann Kafka. He is the businessman who has entrusted his company and all concern for his well-being to his son, as Kafka's father no doubt intended to do. In recognition of the seriousness of this commitment, Georg seeks out the elder Bendemann, for he has just succeeded in making arrangements to relinquish his role of benefactor: he has, first of all, become engaged and has thereby established a measure of independence, and, secondly, he has told his friend in Russia of his intent to lead a life of his own and awaits, somewhat apprehensively, his friend's approval. For the moment, Georg represents the Franz Kafka who had tentatively effected a compromise between the need to write and the need to fulfill the conventional obligations of the bourgeoisie; the meeting with Felice, who had become acquainted with him as the writer Franz Kafka, had enabled him to anticipate bringing about a satisfactory combination of marriage, together with raising and supporting a family, and writing. Acting the part of Herrmann Kafka, the elder Bendemann immediately rejects as invalid the supposition, on which Kafka's plan is based, that Georg has a friend in Russia, namely, that Franz is a writer. Georg tries to reassure his father of his loyalty and to avoid his wrath.

In the midst of the realism which has dominated the delineation of this situation, although the element of Georg's anxiety about his friend is patently hyperbolic, the bizarre intrudes and perseveres to the story's surrealistic conclusion. With a resounding "No" like a thunderbolt from heaven, the old man revives and takes control, mocking both the engagement by defaming the fiancée and the existence of the Russian recluse by making him his ally. This destructive act on his father's part represents the vengeance which the protagonist in "The State of Misery" had forbidden his opponent to enjoy. In "The Judgment" victory belongs to the father, but only apparently so since Georg's friend, whose existence is at stake, survives for the moment. It is the faithful son Georg who dies.

The surfeit of paradoxes which this turn of events produces achieves creditability within the work's province of fiction because of the heightening of the symbolism in the final scene. The ailing young man in Russia, at one point the writer Franz Kafka, becomes, according to Kafka's own interpretation (Journals, p. 296), a metaphor for the relationship between the father and the son. He represents, so Kafka insists, their only point of contact; in other words, the one human bond between them is their dispute over the son's vocation. In the story's denouement, the judgment, that is, the father's verdict, takes the form of a symbolic act, and the son's suicide shows his acceptance of the fact that he has been rejected as a son by his father. The elder Bendemann's remark that Georg's friend is a son after his own heart affords Georg his bitterest moment since he appreciates the irony it is intended to convey. In converting the "character" of the friend in Russia, Kafka's other self, into an aspect of the basic situation in the novella, Kafka has provided himself with an occasion for enlarging the role of the father; he, too, becomes, in the story's climax, a part of the premise on which the fiction rests. More than the father, he is the opposing self of the protagonist. Kafka's conviction which led him to write "The Judgment," as the title itself reveals, was that he was confronting a moral dilemma; if he became a writer, he would be a traitor to his family. The severity of the condemnation of his aspiration to be a writer indicates the workings of that component of the personality which Freud called the super-ego, which can also conveniently be called, in theological terms, the conscience. In this light the father becomes another Doppelgänger; putting the writer in himself, the id, on trial (pertinent is the fact that "Urteil" is related to "ordeal"), Kafka, the super-ego, sentences himself as Georg, the ego and necessarily the totality of his selves, to death. Paradoxically, as unfailingly the paradox appears, the writer for whose sake Georg must disappear survives and triumphs in the form of the story which the conflict and its resolution produced. As a matter of fact, the further adventures of the writer, the vermin which is the id, are chronicled in "Metamorphosis" ("Die Verwandlung").

The multiple fragmentation of the self, occurring in place of a plot in "The Judgment," marks it as an archetypal piece of modern fiction. In a world in which identity is transitory at best (cf. the cult of behaviorism in psychology or Brecht's Mann ist Mann), the individual can gain no foothold, can establish no steady relationship to reality. Fiction mirrors or, better, consists of his perplexity: "The self, if it can be represented at all, must be pictured as forever changing, a consciousness beset with inescapable contradictions, a consciousness of something outside that remains incognizable."[10]

The depiction of a multiplicity of selves, desperately seeking cohesion, as the basis for a work of fiction suffices in regard to the short form of the genre--the story, the novella, the anecdote; however, in the truly epic proportions of the novel the principle of a series of such fragmentations of the personality cannot prevail; the result would have to be mere repetitiousness. Hermann Hesse has afforded some proof of the accuracy of this conclusion in that his novel Der Steppenwolf, a prime example of a portrait of schizophrenic modern man, consists of three sections which explore the same material, only from different vantage points. Therefore, Kafka never accomplished the task of making an entity of his novels; they have a musical rather than a literary quality, consisting of endless variations on a theme. They are necessarily unfinished, and Kafka probably recognized the unsuitability of his talent for accomplishments in the novel form. Perhaps the symbol of the acrobatic singing dogs in "The Research Project of a Dog" ("Forschungen eines Hundes") could be borrowed to represent the writers of the novel because the canine protagonist in this story, who is Kafka, is clearly enthralled by their capabilities, which he can only emulate in an inadequate fashion. [11] He does not perform; he does research. The first of Kafka's three novels, One Who Vanished (Der Verschollene), which now has the not inappropriate title of <u>Amerika</u>, however, exhibits an initial attempt on Kafka's part to conform to the principles on which the epic form is based--plot, character, social background--and their development. Several times, in fact, he attested to the Dickensian dimensions of the projected book (e.g., <u>Journals</u>, p. 535 f.). Nonetheless, <u>One Who Vanished</u> (<u>Amerika</u>) is, in effect, an opening chapter and its elaboration.

"The Stoker" ("Der Heizer"), the first section of the novel, was eventually extracted and published separately; its appearance in print was the mark of approval which Kafka afforded it. Not unexpectedly, its title is significant: it characterizes the theme of the novel, vocation or the search for vocation. The fact that the stoker fulfills his function in the depths of the ship, where it is always night, points to the parallelism between his occupation and the one which Kafka pursued nocturnally and one which he must have felt had a similar importance in propelling the "ship of life"--writing. Hidden in the submerged part of the vessel, the stoker can also represent the id. The protagonist, the ego aspect of the narrator (the story is told in the third person), finds the stoker by accident and in bed. The intruder, who has plumbed the depths by following staircase after staircase downward, is, however, not exclusively a symbol but has some of the attributes of a character in a novel. Conspicuously in the Kafka canon, he has a full name: Karl Rossmann. Kafka's use of names is always deliberate and literary: they are sometimes clearly symbolic, sometimes allusive and sometimes openly autobiographical. In this instance, the "K" in Karl has been assumed to be Kafka's signature: his novelistic protagonists are subsequently Josef K. and K. Linguistically Karl has a relationship to "churl," and the name might refer to Rossmann's status as an outsider. On the other hand, since Kafka was fond of associating his oppressed characters, by way of paradox, with the powerful, with monarchs in particular, he may have been alluding to the Emperor Charles, for whom the German university and a famous bridge in Prague were named. A literary reference is likewise not remote, for the two antithetical brothers, the good one and the bad one, in Schiller's <u>The Robbers</u> (better: <u>The Bandits</u>, <u>Die Räuber</u>) are Karl and Franz. In choosing Rossmann, that is, horseman, to follow "Karl," Kafka was, of course, indulging in his favorite form of metaphor, the conversion of man into beast; in one of the <u>Country Doctor</u> stories, the protagonist is a horse--he is "The New Prosecutor." Since Karl's predicament has come about because his lack of aggres-

siveness has produced evidence of his virility in that he has been se-
duced by a servant girl who becomes pregnant, paradox, as usual, runs
riot.

Sent into exile by his parents because of this indiscretion, Rossmann
arrives in the land of limitless opportunity. But the first sight his eyes
encounter symbolizes frustration: it is the Statue of Liberty, whose
upraised arm holds not enlightenment's torch, but the ancient sword
of divine justice. In order to acquire a vocation, Karl will have to
justify beforehand his right to have pursued it. This inversion of a
logical relationship, the justification of an act which precedes the act
itself, probably the core principle in Kafka's Weltanschauung, applies
most fittingly to the situation of the writer: only by writing can he establish what his calling is, and yet the evidence he advances remains
by its very nature forever suspect. The stoker's quandary is a similar
one; attempting to prove himself a good stoker, he is constantly frustrated by the fact that he must disprove, first of all, the accusations
of Schubal, his foreman,[12] who has automatically assumed the validity of the opposite of that which the stoker might wish to contend.

Irrationally but instinctively, since the ego can but identify with the
id, Karl puts himself (literally) on the side of the stoker, like the
protagonist in "The State of Misery" who defends his ghost, and Georg
Bendemann, who defends his friend in Russia. The story also progres-
ses along the lines established by its predecessors; after the confrontation between the two selves, the overt and the hidden, there is an
encounter with an agent of the super-ego; the father figure appears. In
"The Stoker" he is multiple: Schubal to an extent, then consecutively
the head purser, the captain and Karl's uncle. Before these representatives of "discipline," not "justice," as the text carefully points out,
Karl's defense of the stoker evolves into a self-defense, since he now
feels called upon to make clear his reasons for having taken up the
stoker's cause. The revelation that one of the gentlemen in the captain's cabin is his Uncle Jakob, his only relative in America, who has
moreover been awaiting his arrival, results in Karl's being completely
frustrated in his endeavors and, consequently, in his taking flight in
phantasy, here the advent of the savior. Once again, the supposed de-
feat of the id or the expression of the impossibility of justifying the
existence of the writer has a paradoxical aftermath: the writer triumphs
in that he manipulates event and creates an illogical world (cf., ultimately, the Nature Theater of Oklahoma). At the end of "The Judgment"

Georg dies; at the end of "The Stoker" Karl goes off with his uncle: it is all the same.

However, the novel must continue. Uncle Jakob now becomes a symbol similar to that of the Statue of Liberty, wielding a sword. Living in his house, Karl tries to construct a <u>raison</u> <u>d'être</u> by acquiring pragmatic skills; he learns how to speak English, how to ride a horse and how to activate a mechanical desk, the most appropriate metaphor for the reverse of creative writing. But the efforts to placate the father image, the super-ego, prove to be only the subterfuge of the id; eventually, the fervor of Karl's devotion to his uncle's principles, which approaches cold calculation, alienates the older man; the two scenes which constitute this episode in the progress of the pilgrim Karl, one in his uncle's home, the other in Pollunder's, represent the positive and the negative of the same situation. The happenings of the day in the one become the misadventures of the night in the other. First Karl is petted; then he is persecuted. The descent to the id is as rapid as the country doctor's trip to his patient in that story. Karl's quick acceptance of the invitation of Uncle Jakob's colleague Pollunder to visit his country estate betrays a desire to flee from the whip of discipline and, at the same time, a desire to lash out at the father-figure, symbol also of the will as opposed to the emotions.

In the dark recesses of Mr. Pollunder's rambling house, Karl is plundered of every bright hope of achieving competence in the vocation toward which Uncle Jakob has directed him. In place of the bachelor uncle, a double-figure now commands the scene, part father (Pollunder), part roué (the dinner guest Green). The sexual element, particularly in the form of bisexuality, predominates, signifying in Kafka's metaphoric language the irrational, the realm of the writer. While Pollunder fondles Karl, Green pursues Pollunder's daughter Klara. She in turn first flirts with Karl and then attacks him. Lying in wait, or specifically in bed, is the lascivious groom Mack, in the daytime Karl's friend and tutor and now, after dark, Klara's lover. When Karl attempts to escape from these incarnations of the rampaging libido, he finds his path blocked by Green, whose form grows to the proportions of Mr. Bendemann in his bed or of the groom emerging from the pigsty in "A Country Doctor." Once again, as in "The Judgment," the story comes to a close with the father's rejection of the son, [13] since Green, in Uncle Jakob's own words, his "best friend," at this point delivers to Karl his uncle's letter of dismissal and farewell. The pattern is accordingly complete: in the chapters dealing with Uncle Jakob, named after the patriarch who wrestled with the angel and won a blessing, Kafka has reused the format of a confrontation between an ego and an alter ego, the good Karl and the disobedient, obstinate Karl, followed by the rendering of a verdict--expulsion from paradise. With the wreckage which the id has left around him, but with the facilities for continuing his search restored to him, his cabin-trunk and his umbrella, Karl turns his back on Mr. Pollunder's country house. Outside, in the shadows, lurk Robinson and Delamarche, the ever-resilient id, the inexhaustible source of the writer's creativeness.

It is Kafka's inventiveness which characterizes his fiction and which sustains One Who Vanished despite its simplistic structure, its repetitiousness. Because of the ingenuity of Kafka's metaphors, which lend themselves to a myriad of interpretations, the epic intent and quality of his work has not always been acknowledged. In pursuing an aspect of the symbolism in the Kafka canon and its significance, this study does not purpose to establish that he had any other object than that of creating a body of fiction; in particular, there is no assumption that his work is allegorical. To the contrary. In reference to One Who Vanished, in which there clearly are sociological overtones, Heinz Politzer stresses Kafka's novelistic point of view: "Yet Kafka the novel writer was not concerned with prophecy but with the literary validity of the images he produced."[14] The two episodes in One Who Vanished which follow Karl's eviction from Pollunder's estate are basically the further adventures of a peculiar kind of Gulliver in a world, the reality, not the unreality of which is vividly imagined. The underlying metaphorical pattern which this study purpots to find is but one of the many subtleties interwoven, some deliberately, some inadvertantly, in the fabric of a work of fiction. The dichotomous selves, prevelant in the earlier chapters, the ego-oriented protagonist and his double, that is, the phantom-ridden writer and recluse, are prominent alternately in the book's closing chapters. In the Hotel Occidental section of the novel the extroverted Karl Rossmann seeks success in the workaday world; in the Brunelda narrative Karl Rossmann's hidden self has the lead.

Karl's attempt to establish himself in a vocation begins in an atmosphere bright with good omens. The name of the hotel, where he readily finds employment as an elevator operator, may be a subtle reference by Kafka to the part of the Jewish nation well assimilated in Western Europe, of whose number Kafka's father was one. For the Westeners, Eastern Jewry constituted an alien race, enveloped in religious mysticism. Replacing Frieda Brandenfeld as a symbol of the expectation of success, two women (another doubling) appear, the hotel manageress and her very young secretary, whose overt function (there is another aspect) is to ensure that Karl will prosper in his new career. But even before their good influence can take effect, the ubiquitous agent of the id, the representation of the fatal flaw, formerly the ghost, the friend in Russia, later the insect, the wound, et al., has made its presence known. In this instance, two symbolic figures play the one role. Kafka's use of the device of duality has received considerable attention from literary critics. Charles Neider in The Frozen Sea and elsewhere has drawn attention to a lengthy series of such pairings[15] and has concluded that Kafka's proclivity for the employment of the concept of two reveals his awareness of his peculiar isolation, his oneness. A different analysis of the phenomenon occurs in H. Platzer Collins' article "Kafka's 'Double-Figure' as a Literary Device" (Monatshefte, LV, January, 1963), where the identical natures of the pairs is stressed to the end that the doubles would seem to provide Kafka with a chorus who can comment on his protagonist's activities. However, Kafka's unmistakable preference for the Doppelgänger motif, his attachment to it, derived as it no doubt is from a personal acquaintanceship with the experience of doubling, being physically beside one's self, and also, very likely, from a fondness for the stories of E. T. A. Hoffmann, suggests a stronger, a fundamental involvement with the metaphor. In One Who Vanished, Karl Rossmann's hidden self has the form of two vagabonds (accordingly, one is called Delamarche),[16] who have a common cause in the novel but who are furthermore different aspects of the same nature (e. g., homosexuality and heterosexuality). In plundering his trunk, they ruin Karl's credentials. Their early appearance foreshadows Karl's failure in his new undertaking, whatever it may be. Even Karl's sponsors, who, because they are women, play a prototypally ambiguous part, are harbingers of Karl's downfall. Therese, for one, named after a saint, a legendary figure, tells the story of her mother, excluded from society because she has no employment, doomed to commit suicide, somewhat like Georg Bendemann. At the crucial moment, the manageress falls victim to the irrationality of her sexual nature and, because of her love for the head waiter, abandons Karl. Previously, the ego aspect of Karl Rossmann, who has had a measure of success in his position as elevator operator, has persevered. With the reappearance of Robinson, Karl's disreputable "friend" or self, the story enters upon its second phase, depicting the disruptive effect of the id, the anomalous element in the personality. Finally, as usual in Kafka, there is the confrontation with the super-ego, the conscience, the figure of the father. He is, conspicuously in this regard, two people, the head waiter and the head porter, the first a lover, the second a disciplinarian; however, both are involved as one in the process of condemnation--the dismissal of Karl.

The penultimate episode in One Who Vanished, before its "key" chapter, takes place in the nether world of phantasy and sexuality, which the writer must plumb in order to be able to give his work the aspect of truth, to provide it with a depth which removes it from the shallowness of being entertainment. Through the machinations of Robinson and Delamarche Karl becomes the thrall of Brunelda. Since this figure of a woman has the ambiguous outlines of the Kafkaesque symbol, the variety of interpretations it has produced is considerable: its size, considered in the light of Kafka's fondness for animal metaphor, suggests the queen bee or the queen of the ant colony; in this guise it can readily represent capitalism--immobile, indolent,   living off the feverish activity of the workers. Man's enslavement to his sexual nature can easily be taken to be the label which Kafka intended to affix to the character of Brunelda, since the plot of this episode revolves around the sexual appetites of Brunelda and the men around her. What has been frequently overlooked, however, in attempting to analyze Brunelda's function in the novel, is her vocation: she is an opera singer, namely, an artist--therefore, the Wagnerian name, with its similarity to Brunnhilde. Excluded from the "normal" world of work and family life because of his inclination toward Bohemian eccentricity, Karl is forced to join in the disorderly, almost criminal behavior of those living in the shadows. In Brunelda's apartment, Karl makes unhappy discoveries about himself, because, for Kafka, writing entailed self-confrontation, facing a divine or absolute judgment. In Brunelda's lover, Delamarche, Karl begins to see his heterosexual self as his "worst enemy." Rather, he discovers, he is to follow in the footsteps or paw-prints of Robinson, who compares himself to a dog, living in a state of frustration and homoerotic impulses. Behind the metaphoric treatment of these events, in which the similes are almost exclusively sexual, towers the imposing theme of the artist's dilemma: as a writer Kafka must relinquish his hope of combining marriage and a career with commitment to his true vocation. Among the many mirror images, self-portraits, which line the pages of the Brunelda chapter, one depicts the real Kafka--it is the "student" Josef Mendel, who describes as his routine of study the daily routine of Franz Kafka, bureaucrat and writer, and who advises Karl that he "absolutely" must keep his humiliating post in Brunelda's apartment. The conversation between the two outcasts takes place between balconies, Karl having taken refuge from his three oppressors on the balcony. Once again, in choosing the scene, used frequently in the Brunelda episode, Kafka shows himself to be preoccupied with self-revelation; in an autobiographical comment elsewhere he has recalled the shock of being, as a child, locked out on the balcony of his parents' bedroom in punishment for having annoyed them--particularly his father. Kafka can escape neither the memory nor the exclusion and isolation to which his writer's calling dooms him, and so Karl Rossmann remains forever Brunelda's prisoner: Kafka never found an ending for the chapter. There are intimations, both in the episode itself and in the draft of a continuation, that Karl was to have yet another opportunity to solve the enigma which his life had become.

While a solution to Karl's problem, his enslavement, is not forthcoming in the "real" world of America, Kafka has supplied, in the novel's final, although unfinished chapter, a phantasy, in which the ambiguity of Karl's vocation is resolved. The suddenness of Karl's release marks the magical character of the situation; much as Hermann Hesse's Steppenwolf finds the door to his "magic theater" miraculously explosed in a brick wall, so Karl Rossmann precipitously, perhaps in an unguarded moment, stumbles across a sign announcing that membership in the Nature Theater of Oklahoma is open to all: that is, anyone who wants to be an artist may join. The paradoxical nature of the concept which Kafka proposes as the answer to the riddle of the writer's lack of status becomes clear in the choice of the name Oklahoma. It means "the beautiful country," which bears the connotation of "heaven." To bolster further the supposition that only in another life will art be recognized as a genuine craft, Kafka designates the race track at Clayton as the assembly point for candidates for membership in the theatrical company; as Norbert Fürst has pointed out, Clayton, town of clay, signifies the grave. [17] And when Karl arrives in Clayton, a welcome is trumpeted out by a band of angels. One of them is Fanny, apparently someone of whom Karl had been particularly fond in the past. Since Fanny begins with "F," as Karl does with "K," the assumption follows that Fanny represents Felice, at least in the significance she had for Kafka in regard to his aspiration to be a writer. Fanny admits Karl to the inner circle at the track; thereby Kafka realizes his dream of marriage to Felice combined with a literary career. Another symbol for this euphoric prospect is the family group, Mr. Kala, his wife and, in a perambulator, their child, who simultaneously with Karl, seek employment from the theater representatives in the Clayton pavilion. All are successful, and Karl is overjoyed when he recognizes another artist who has been engaged--Giacomo, the child-like liftboy of the Hotel Occidental. On the one hand, Giacomo resembles the child-ghost of "The State of Misery," and therefore suggests the hidden self, the writer; [18] on the other hand, his name is the diminutive of Jakob so that, in having Giacomo at his side, Karl would appear to have regained the favor and affection of his uncle. In these figures and events, projecting a resolution of all conflicts, Kafka devised both a key to his novel (in the same sense that "Before the Law" is a key to The Trial) and to the puzzle of the writer's dual nature, in this respect a fictitious key. He has also, once more, brought his story to a conclusion by letting the id, the creative unconscious, triumph, while the ego, here Karl Rossmann, condemned to enslavement by the multiple agents of the super-ego, languishes in the limbo of New York. This prevailing fixed sequence of events in Kafka's early work, it must be pointed out, must have evolved subconsciously and intuitively for him, since the Freudian tripartite self had not yet, at that time, become dogma. But then it is one of Kafka's great feats as a writer that his work anticipates history.

Chapter II - Footnotes

[1] I have used the dates pertaining to when the items were written and published provided in Franz Kafka: Dichter über ihre Dichtungen.

[2] Franz Kafka: Erzählungen und kleine Prosa. New York 1946; p. 17. Further references appear in the text under the rubric Stories.

[3] "Die Deutbarkeit von Kafkas Werken" in: Heinz Politzer, ed.: Franz Kafka. Darmstadt 1973; p. 416.

[4] Anthony Thorlby: Kafka: a Study. London 1972; p. 6.

[5] Hochzeitsvorbereitungen auf dem Lande, p. 12.

[6] Beschreibung einer Form. München 1968; p. 54.

[7] Begegnung mit dem Nichts. München 1950; p. 173. Cf. Kurt Fickert: Kafka's "In the Penal Colony." In: The Explicator 24 (September 1965); item 11.

[8] The name Georg may refer either to St. George who slays the mythical beast or to Kafka's brother Georg who died in infancy and whose role he has assigned to himself.

[9] A. P. Foulkes: The Reluctant Pessimist. The Hague 1967; p. 100.

[10] Charles I. Glicksberg: The Self in Modern Literature. University Park, Pa., 1963; p. xii.

[11] Cf. Wilhelm Emrich, Franz Kafka, p. 62: "This research project of a dog does indeed reflect Kafka's own literary experimentation."

[12] Heinz Politzer: Franz Kafka: Parable and Paradox. Ithaca, N.Y., 1962; p. 310. He suggests that the name Schubal is derived from "Schubiak," meaning a rogue or "a man who stands in everybody's way." The latter interpretation would be apt in the light of the fact that Kafka is fond of deliberately misnaming his characters (cf. Huld); it is Karl who is in the way.

[13] A detail which deserves attention is the name Mack, which means "son." Mr. Bendemann, it should be noted, berates his son for having fallen victim to Frieda Brandenfeld's sexual advances.

[14] Franz Kafka: Parable and Paradox, p. 124.

[15] The Frozen Sea. New York 1962; p. 29. Also "The Cabalists" in: Angel Flores, ed.: The Kafka Problem. New York 1946; p. 419.

[16] Robinson (Crusoe) is a traveler, too, and in addition leads a shipwrecked, insular existence.

[17] Die offenen Geheimtüren Franz Kafkas, p. 54.

[18] Notably, Italian names and/or connotations in Kafka's work indicate the realm of the abstract--the spiritual, the cerebal, the imaginative. The association of Italy with art and religion is an obvious one.

CHAPTER III

At the Office and at the Bar of Justice

At one time (cf. <u>Letters</u>, p. 116) Kafka considered combining "The
Judgment," "The Stoker" and "Metamorphosis" ("Die Verwandlung")
in one volume which would be called <u>Sons</u> (Söhne). Even more significant
in the relationship between the three works than the obvious fact that
the protagonists are sons in conflict with their fathers and/or families
is the variety Kafka achieves in elaborating the theme common to them
all. In "The Judgment" the confrontation between the forces of conscience or moral probity and the person burdened with a secret self
ends precipitously in the extinction of the total personality. The protagonist is rescued in "The Stoker" gratuitously, by an act of provi-
dence. But the most shocking turn of events, certainly one of the most
shocking in all fiction, occurs in "Metamorphosis," which Kafka
wrote in November, 1912, while the flood of inspiration continued
unabated which his meeting with Felice had released. In a bold ex-
pansion of the use of metaphor Kafka fashioned an entire story out
of a death sentence; upon the exposure of his hidden self, the protagonist in "Metamorphosis" is doomed to exterminate it and with
it, himself. This time Kafka's literary double has the name of Gregor
Samsa, "Samsa" being an obvious approximation of "Kafka" and "Gregor" perhaps an allusion to the legendary Gregorius, the holy sinner,
who after bouts of incest and penance becomes pope. Samsa's com-
placent acceptance of his life as successful salesman and family breadwinner comes to a sudden end in a moment of revelation, of self-discovery, which takes place as he awakens one morning. The staid bourgeois, the epitome of the unreflective mind, takes a long, deep look
at himself and discovers his fearsome counterpart. What has suddenly
appeared is a huge insect, a form of vermin. It is a form of existence
which is twice cursed, since it is the expression of both the incapacity
to lead a "normal" life and the vilification which this aberrance entails. Metaphorically labeled something less than human by society
and psychologically convinced of his baseness and depravity, the writer in Kafka emerges from the cocoon of Kafka, the dutiful son and com-
petent bureaucrat, now entirely an insect. In the first part of the story
the metamorphosed protagonist contends with his cast-off self. The
argument between the young man and his child-ghost, as in "The State
of Misery," is repeated in other terms; Georg Bendemann's hesitancy

to inform his friend in Russia reappears. The insect which Gregor
Samsa has become tries to reassure first of all himself, then his parents, his sister and eventually a representative of the firm which employs him that nothing has changed, that he will still make his train and
proceed with his life as a salesman. His protestations, like Georg
Bendemann's, fail because the truth of the situation is immediately
apparent. It, in the form of Gregor's obnoxious hidden self, repels
both his family and his business associate. The agent of his conscience,
his sense of justice, present in the person of Gregor's father, takes
charge of matters, and, wielding the business superior's cane in one
hand and a newspaper in the other (like the newspaper in "The Judgment"
a sign of authority), drives the insect back into concealment.

The middle section in the story's tripartite structure deals with the
family's tolerance of the stranger in their midst. There is a reprieve
for the insect. But, once again, as in the Hotel Occidental episode in
One Who Vanished, it is the ambivalence of the role that women play
in the protagonist's life which destroys the delicate equilibrium main-
tained temporarily in the situation. In general, women comprise for
Kafka the wholly human element in life; they are not seekers after
truth, that is, artists, or embodiments of moral precepts, that is,
the opposition. In their frailty, especially in their sexual, rather than
intellectual orientation, they provide Kafka's philosopher-kings with
solace when they have to confront their own weaknesses and with obstacles which they must surmount in order to be able to acquire true
insight. In "Metamorphosis" Gregor's mother and sister--named
Grete, a variant of Gretel, as if to emphasize her capacity to minis-
ter to her brother--undertake the mission of making Gregor more
comfortable in his writer's seclusion. But their all too human concern
takes on the aspect of being interference with and distraction from his
monastic regimen when they try to remove impediments from his path
and deprive him of his seal of election, a photograph of the "muse"
hanging on the wall. In Kafka's paradoxical fashion, this woman in a
fur boa simultaneously represents the sexual relationship which the
artist has foresworn. Misled by the women's attempt to mitigate the
circumstances of his exile, the insect-writer, the hidden self, emerges
in the light and, in a repetition of that which occurs in the story's opening episode, almost immediately encounters the father-figure who pun-
ishes the miscreant by hurling apples at him in a manner which resembles the stoning to death of the criminal. The psychological import
of this scene, of which Kafka may have been only dimly aware, since

"Metamorphosis" is fiction and not a clinical case study, has given rise
to several hyperbolic interpretations of the entire story. [1] One such
Freudian explanation of the surrealistic events of "Metamorphosis"
proposes that Gregor, the prototype of the son, has transformed himself in order to avoid having to commit patricide for the purpose of
replacing his father in the connubial bed; the motif of incest is present, at least subliminally, in the story, and Kafka has himself com-
pared the relationship between brother and sister to that of mother and
father (Journals, p. 290). In this interpretation, the son's submission
to the authority of the father provides the apple-throwing incident with
homosexual overtones. At the same time, since religious connotations,
together with the sexual, are everywhere in the Kafka canon, the apples in "Metamorphosis" can be considered a central image in a canvas
which depicts everyman's (Gregor's) expulsion from the Garden of Eden
at the behest of God the Father as a consequence of his "guilt," a comprehension of which is patently a motivating factor in Gregor's case.

Condemned for all these reasons--his nonconformity, his murderous
intent toward his father and his sinful nature, the protagonist carries
out the order of execution on himself in the story's final section. He
becomes the victim of starvation and the "wound," incurred when an
apple, lodged in his scales during the attack, putrifies; both symbols,
the inability to ingest food and the wound, figure prominently in Kafka's works (see especially "A Hunger-Artist" and "A Country Doctor")
and are the stigmata of the artist. But before the denouement in "Metamorphosis" there is a final confrontation scene between the inner and
outer selves of Gregor Samsa. In this instance Kafka's use of the doubling motif is somewhat innovative. Three characters, all alike, represent the bourgeois Gregor; they are the boarders whom the Samsa family has taken in in order to supplement an income severely reduced by
Gregor's incapacity to earn money. One evening, Grete plays the violin
to entertain this threefold caricature of propriety, and, enticed from
his hiding place by this homey scene and these melodious sounds, the
insect comes into view. Another fairly common symbol in Kafka, e.g.,
in "The Research Project of a Dog," the music here and elsewhere
indicates the presence of the outsider-artist. The three boarders, who
have not been particularly impressed by the music, are now totally
immersed in escaping from the phenomenon they have encountered.
With a touch of the realism he usually provides at climactic moments,
Kafka indicates that, because they have been routed by the Samsa "mon-
ster," the boarders do not intend to pay any rent. Rejected now by his
bourgeois self and even by his sister, who shuts him up in his room,

in herself a symbol for his ambitions in the field of art, Gregor no longer delays submitting to the dictates of conscience and expires. The story closes on a note of exhileration like that in "The Judgment"; there, the traffic moved briskly over the bridge from which Georg had just hurled himself, and here Grete's young body blossoms forth. This ending also points the way to the last event in "A Hunger-Artist," which concerns the removal of the emaciated figure of the artist and the substitution for it of a sleek and thriving panther. In life, life wins and the death-in-life of the artist becomes literal.

The enthusiasm produced by successfully writing a novella provided Kafka with a basis for another endeavor in the longer epic form, the novel. As the pursuit of Felice took its torturous course, Kafka conceived of yet another way to transliterate event into metaphor. In 1914, probably after the nullification of his engagement to Felice, he began writing The Trial (Der Prozess), in which there is a reversal of the parts played by Kafka and his Doppelgänger; the ego aspect of Kafka, the young man with a good job and with a landlady who approves of him is now the protagonist, while his hidden self accompanies him doggedly, foisting on him the obsession that he is a criminal who has been arrested in secret and must appear at the bar of not earthly, but absolute justice. The arrest, which symbolizes the coming into existence of an awareness of his dichotomous personality, occurs or seems to occur as Josef K. awakens on the morning of his thirtieth birthday. K. is, of course, Kafka's usual signature, perhaps an honest replacement for the fictitious "I"; that is to say, the "I" as the protagonist in a work of fiction is for the most part not autobiographical, whereas K. is really Kafka, as seen by the writer Kafka. The choice of "Josef" has been explained in various ways: it suggested itself to Kafka either because, as a Jew, he wanted to name himself ironically after the Jewish ghetto of Prague, Josefstadt, or because, as a petty official in the Austrian bureaucracy, his real first name seemed to demand doubling into Franz-Josef as in the case of the Austrian Emperor, or because, as a writer, he associated Josef with the Biblical Josef, who had become the prototype of the artist in the literature of the early twentieth century.

There are two officers of the court outside Josef K.'s bedroom, waiting to arrest him as soon as he arises. The doubling has its usual significance as a sign of the antithetical nature of his personality; one of the officers is Franz. Symbolizing the other self, the overt self, three representatives of the bank for which Josef K. works are also present in his rooms and act as observers of the arrest; in addition, their names suggest a relationship with the protagonist: Kaminer, Kullich (both with "K") and Rabensteiner (in "Wedding Preparations" the variant "Raban" initially appears). It is obvious that an existentialistic confrontation has taken place in the mind of Josef K. Perhaps the morning of his thirtieth birthday represents a crucial moment in his life, one which requires that Josef K. take account of himself. Has he been leading a double life so that Josef K., whose personality consists of his clothes, lives routinely in the bounds of convention, while a shadow Josef K., who reflects on the meaninglessness of the first Josef's existence, waits for admittance just outside the nearest door? The activity of the arrest soon spills over into the bedroom of Fräulein Bürstner, another boarder, who seems to have special significance for Josef K. Her initials reveal that in this instance Kafka refers to Felice Bauer and is analyzing their relationship. (Bürstner also has vulgar connotations.) Since the arrest is the recognition of his two selves, Kafka now relates F.B. to them both; her life has been intruded upon by his very personal dilemma. Having discovered that his arrest does not entail appearing before a magistrate, that it, in fact, changes nothing, Josef K. determines to confront Fräulein Bürstner in the evening, after he has returned from work. Before seeing her, he becomes involved in a conversation with his landlady, Frau Grubach, who brings a quixotic human note to these events rife with ciphers instead of characters. Like Samsa's mother and sister, Frau Grubach in her befuddled way wants to help the protagonist but, instead, puts obstacles in his path. She is suspicious of Fräulein Bürstner, whom Josef K. expects to play a key role in freeing him from his enslavement to routine--Kafka's mother once persuaded him to hire a detective in Berlin to look into Felice's past and reputation. Already unsure and now disconcerted about the nature of his attitude toward Fräulein Bürstner, Josef K. brings their brief rendezvous, which has begun promisingly, to a ruinous end: he overwhelms her with his advances. The destructive force which the sexual element in a relationship can exert impressed Kafka particularly so that he concluded in his Journals (p. 315) that coitus was a punishment for the joy of being in love and together. In this light, Kafka's hope of combining a career as a writer with a bourgeois existence through marriage to Felice was doomed, and The Trial's first chapter concludes with its protagonist completely frustrated.

Subsequently, all his efforts to deal with his arrest are futile. It is the "arrested" part (paradoxically, since his bourgeois self is truly arrested) who next endeavors to deal with the total Josef K.'s dilemma by justifiying his existence to the court. That Kafka has now arrived at the stage in his writing when he is able to transcend the realm of private confession, embellished by striking metaphors, becomes obvious. Here there is a concentration on a philosophic problem, which was conspicuously lacking, for example, in "Description of a Struggle." The particular case of Josef K., pertinent in the Fräulein Bürstner episode, recedes in the background, while he becomes a prototype of thinking man, the intellectual, with the intellect divided into the observer and the observed. Kafka's purpose in continuing the story is less to establish an equilibrium for Josef K. than to probe the basic problem of the meaningfulness of life, its justification. Bede Allemann has, indeed, summarized all of Kafka's work in this regard: "In his writing only one single question is put, but put in as fundamental a fashion as possible: the question of a raison d'être (Existenzfrage), which thematically becomes the problem of the justification of existence."[2] Before the court, which is in itself invisible but which is represented by life, a random assortment of the young and the old, the concerned and the bored, the conscientious and the lascivious, Josef K., the awakened or arrested Sunday self, not the workaday self, makes a plea to be excused from participating in this trial, this purposeless pursuit of justice. No one knows what he is talking about, of course, and there is chaos. When he attempts on a subsequent occasion to reappear before the court to resume his arguments, he finds that what he had considered to be a session of the court had been his interpretation of a scene in which life was proceeding as usual; now, having made this discovery, he becomes involved in the intimate activities which constitute the outward appearance of the court and subsequently finds himself in its offices, on its periphery. Oppressed by the atmosphere of lassitude and suffering he encounters as he makes his way closer to the court's philosophic center--the insolubility of the riddle of life,[3] Josef K. feels faint and leaves.

In the two chapters which follow, in Brod's ordering of the chapters, Josef K. still deals directly and personally with the consequences of his arrest; for the remainder of the novel he will be involved with intermediaries. As if in anticipation of this indirect approach to finding a way out of his dilemma and the resultant frustration, Kafka returns to K.'s involvement with Fräulein Bürstner by depicting an interview with her representative, another woman residing in the boarding house, Fräulein Montag--the name indicates some opposition to the Sunday activities of Josef K. and also contains a verbal echo of Dafoe's

52

Robinson Crusoe (the protagonist's man "Friday"), of which Kafka was patently fond. Playing the usual part assigned to women in the Kafka canon, Fräulein Montag gives voice to her concern for Josef K., to her good intentions toward him, all the while placing obstacles in the way of his achieving a modus vivendi in his relationship with Fräulein Bürstner. In assuming the role of good conscience, which would spare Fräulein Bürstner an embroilment in K.'s difficulties, she is joined by Captain Lanz, whose name carries at least a suggestion of the sword of justice and also of the virility which K. lacks. Together, Fräulein Montag and Captain Lanz bring to an end K.'s endeavors to reach a solution to his problems by means of the intercession of Fräulein Bürstner. The pair has a certain biographical import in that Kafka did indeed have two friends, one, Grete Bloch, Felice Bauer's confidante, and the other, Ernst Weiss, Kafka's self-appointed advisor, who sought to prevent further embarrassment to Franz Kafka and Felice Bauer in their unhappy engagement. In removing Fräulein Bürstner from the scene of K.'s combat with the dichotomy which he must master, Kafka takes another step in the direction of dealing with general concepts rather than specific instances.

The split between his two natures, the one oriented to the world, to marriage, to a career, and the other oriented to the spirit, to the absolute, to literature, finds symbolic expression in the reappearance of K.'s two warders, the arresting officers. Josef K. stumbles on them in a basement room in the bank in which he works; thus the simultaneous functioning of routine and of the court in K.'s life becomes apparent. In Franz and Willem, named to indicate an authority which they pretend to exercise while lacking it, Kafka presents another instance of the employment of the literary device to which he is partial--the double, for the two bailiffs are, on the one hand, indistinguishable from one another and symbolize the same concept, that of the court, while, on the other hand, they are individualized, with different names and different backgrounds (one is married, one is not--Franz, as a matter of fact, whose bride is waiting for him at the door of the bank). While this specific instance of doubling in The Trial is of minor import, the use of the device in The Castle, in the appearance of K.'s assistants, Artur and Jeremias, has great significance in regard to the structure of the entire novel. In this scene in The Trial the pair of warders obviously serve to evoke a picture of Josef K.'s ambivalent attitude toward his arrest, his incapacity to lead a "normal" life. He discovers them as they are stripped and put to the whip; the sadism in the episode can but reflect Kafka's conviction that the pursuit of esoteric goals entails exploration of forbidden, libidinous territory. The punishment of the warders is the work of Josef K.'s conscience which abhors the ir- regularity of his aspiration to be more than a dutiful bureaucrat. But he refuses to interpret the event of the whipping at all and simply shuts the door on the execution of punishment; Norbert Fürst has characterized it as Josef K.'s "nightmare."[4] His "arrest" is now irreversible. At this point Josef K.'s efforts to deal with his predic- ament turn desperate. Matters are no longer in his hands: he acts through intermediaries of the court through intermediaries who have been brought to his attention by other intermediaries. Peopling his novels with these characters who exist only in their relationship to Josef K. and his problem, Kafka gives evidence of the ego-splitting that is, decomposition, which has resulted from his struggle to achieve antithetical accomplishments, fulfillment in literature and fulfillment in everyday life. This Romantic preoccupation with the writer's self invariably produces a confrontation between the dif- ferent aspects of an incohesive personality. In general, Kurt Wein- berg's dictum prevails: "Almost all minor figures in Kafka's stories are [...] the embodiments of <u>concepts</u> in the hero's mind, [as] ac- companying phenomena (<u>Begleiterscheinungen</u>)."[5] Having established the basic premise, Kafka now begins his elaborate analysis of it, proceeding by examining numerous speculations about the "arrest" and methods of dealing with it, which are personified, since Kafka is im- pelled to write a work of fiction.

While Kafka's Uncle Rudolf actually sought to intercede in his nephew's affairs in order to be of assistance to him, Kafka introduces an Uncle Karl in his novel (later called Albert--another royal name), who is the materialization of Josef K.'s sensitivity to his predicament, namely, his enslavement to routine and the compulsion of his need to escape. Uncle Karl presents K. to the lawyer Huld--the name symbolism is as significant as it is paradoxical. On the assumption that the protagonist in the novel is guilty because he has instituted the conflict within the self, a failing for which his conscience has already condemned him, Kafka concerns himself, first of all, with the idea of obtaining divine dispensation: grace or "Huld." But the personification of this concept is a befuddled, bed-ridden advocate. And his advice, largely negative in character, imbued with fogginess and the black of frustration, is overlooked as Josef K. finds himself involved with the sickly lawyer's nurse, Leni. The name identifies the character: Magdalena, the pro- miscuous woman. Typically in Kafka's fiction, she represents the in- trusion of the erotic upon the protagonist's ascetic devotion to a spiritual cause. Furthermore, she is the ubiquitous helpful female who perversely puts stumbling blocks in the hero's path to his sublime destination. Kafka provides her with webbed fingers, as if to emphasize the animalistic nature which motivates her.

As Josef K. becomes more and more preoccupied with his secret life, which simultaneously loses its covertness, and concentrates less and less on his occupation, he is led to speculate further about remedies-- more desperate ones--for the unhappy state of affairs. Emphasizing the public aspect of K.'s sense of shame, Kafka next introduces another intermediary, who is a customer of the bank for which K. works; now not only the intimate world of the family knows of the unsavory situation of his arrest, but the business world is also well-informed about it. Through this new mediator, K. is led to another, the artist Titorelli. Relinquishing the hope for the administration of grace, having previously abandoned the expectation of deliverance through the intercession of Fräulein Bürstner, Josef K. next explores the avenue of creativity which might lead to atonement for his transgression. By symbolizing literature through portraits, Kafka depicts the efforts of the writer to redeem himself in his self-imposed isolation by producing works of art. But Titorelli (the name is an amalgamation of those of several Italian masters, but Weinberg associates it with Titurel) merely paints the same desolate landscape over and over, a prospect which might be equated with the nature of Kafka's stories. There is also a portrait of justice in Titorelli's studio-bedroom, since Kafka's conscience dooms in advance K.'s hope for success in this new endeavor. In the endless duplication of motifs, which, in Kafka's hands, constitutes the structure of the novel, the theme of the ambiguous part which women play in the protagonist's life (cf. Fräulein Bürstner, Fräulein Montag, Leni) is repeated with the appearance of the laughing girls who hover on the periphery of the sudio. For Weinberg, they replace Kundrie. Ultimately, Titorelli's counsel is as disappointing as the ignored Huld's was, perhaps because Josef K. has failed to ask the appropriate questions. Kafka reiterates the previously made point that the individual, torn between an obligation to fulfill an inner need and an obligation to adhere to social dictates, can find no solution. In contradiction to the negativism which persists throughout The Trial, there exists an unfinished chapter, excised from the more or less established text, which portrays a minor triumph for Josef K.: he is escorted to the seat of the law by Titorelli. For a moment, it would appear, Kafka contemplated the possibility of establishing himself and achieving recognition as a writer; but he had to give up this hope as a cruel chimera.

In describing another visit by K. to the lawyer Huld, this time for the purpose of dismissing him from the case, and a long-lasting encounter with another accused, Kafka returns, with even greater intensity, to his contemplation of the hopelessness of his situation. Most critics are in accord in viewing the businessman Block, whose "arrest" has ruined his life to the extent that he now lives it in Huld's shadow, in the lawyer's house, as a projection of what Josef K. would be, should he devote himself exclusively to dealing with the court. Block's stubborn determination to achieve acquittal is implicit in his name, which also carries an overtone of relevance to writing: "Schreibblock," writing tablet. As Kafka explicitly states, the transformation of the lawyer's client into his dog, the symbol of Block's state, is the consequence of the pursuit of self-discovery, and the import of this unfinished chapter is its foreshadowing of the inevitability of Josef K.'s fate, his destiny to die like a dog.

Before the end, he is granted a moment of insight, a glimpse of the significance of his travail, a fleeting look inside the court. Once again, an intermediary introduces an intermediary: an Italian client of the bank puts K. in the path of the prison chaplain. Since the scene of Josef K.'s enlightenment by the chaplain is the candlelight-dim interior of a cathedral, the theological implications of the story of The Trial must be evaluated. Central in considering the issue of the book's religious orientation is an understanding of Kafka's assertion of Josef K.'s "guilt." Equating guilt with a fall from grace or establishing it as the measure of man's distance from God, the interpreter of The Trial is free to conclude that Kafka is close to presenting an allegory about the sinful state of man, according to which Josef K. is an everyman and a pilgrim in search of grace. Because of the book's modernity or because of Kafka's failure to embrace Christianity with its doctrine of the redemptive death of Christ, the protagonist in The Trial dies unforgiven. However, even the nihilism of this conclusion has lent itself to incorporation in an analysis of The Trial as the confession of a faith: "What must a man do to be saved?" is John Kelly's summary of the book's theme. [6] "Kafka works out his hero's problem," he continues, "by basing his allegory on the prophetic writings of the Old Testament and on Calvin's Pauline Christianity, absorbed through Kierkegaard." Max Brod, for another, sees Kafka as a mystic, albeit a very different one from Kierkegaard. The salvation, the absolution from guilt, which Josef K. either receives as his due or dies without, is, in the final analysis, not necessarily identical with that which results from a religious experience. By his own testimony, Kafka's interest in established religion was minimal, and his acquaintanceship with Kierkegaard's work, up to the very last years of his life, was casual.

The import of the cathedral scene and the chaplain's edifying lecture can easily lie outside its trappings, just as the imagery of arrest and trial is devoid of any message pertaining to the legal system in the Hapsburg Empire. As a writer of fiction, Kafka was primarily concerned with the presentation of reality through the use of words, and Josef K.'s crisis of identity could most readily be made comprehensible by employing theological terms, but only as a point of reference. The character Josef K. who enters upon a vista of self-revelation as he hears the chaplain thunder out his name is, after all, that totality of a multitude of selves of Franz Kafka which the writer Franz Kafka has pieced together out of dreams, memories, ruminations and phantasies. Neither the devout believer nor the confirmed skeptic, the Kafka whom the writer has objectified is clearly a troubled man, dubious of his capacity to function both on the level of social interaction and on the level of maintaining the integrity of his personality. Josef K.'s plight is the subject of the chaplain's parable about the man from the country, which contains, by common consent, the sum and substance of The Trial. It tells of two people who exist only in relationship to one another and of a door or gate to the law, before which both are stationed. The law, represented as blinding light, is patently an ideal, the realization of which is, by definition, unattainable. At the same time, the aspiration to realize this ideal motivates, almost exclusively, the one figure, the man from the country, while his counterpart, the door-keeper or gate-keeper exists only in order to constitute an impediment to the fulfillment of his confederate's sole desire. There can be little doubt that in the legend Kafka has reduced to their simplest terms the concepts of negative and positive factors in the fictionalized Franz Kafka, Josef K., which both prevent and foster the formulation of an integrated self. Neither the door-keeper nor the man from the country is more powerful; the chaplain eventually explains that the authority of the door-keeper is only apparent and that the man from the country's control of the situation is intrinsic, although unused. Since Kafka wished his analysis of his personal predicament to be generally applicable, he devised a parable (he published this brief segment of the novel separately), and thereby relieved himself of the necessity of supplying specific instances and unequivocal terminology. He does not identify his ideal or the forces in him which inhibit and promote his progress toward it. The legend becomes a rapidly sketched portrait of the human condition, of man's frailty, his fallibility, his inner conflicts, resulting from his comprehension of a wholeness, a perfection, forever in his sight but beyond his reach.

After this cryptic denouement the novel comes abruptly to an end--it may be that Josef K. was to repeat, because of his failure to understand, the endeavor to circumvent the conditions of his arrest. As it is, the novel is unfinished but has a conclusion. One year after the turmoil in his life began, Josef K. once again receives two visitors in his rooms. This time they are executioners. With Josef K. between them, they march to a stone quarry on the outskirts of the city. On the way K. catches a glimpse of a woman who might be Fräulein Bürstner, but he makes no attempt to contact her. His resignation to the hopelessness of his situation is complete. The autobiographical import of this final reference to Fräulein Bürstner involves consideration of the significance to Kafka of his engagement to Felice Bauer and its dissolution. The ill-omened affair, he must have felt, was the one courageous act he had performed in his life, his rebellion against a fate which decreed that he must be unhappy, half a writer, half a capable, well-functioning human being. But this supreme effort to achieve balance had been foiled. In the mood of fathomless dejection which ensued, he conceived of Josef K.'s final hour. Enervated by the almost endless series of bouts with the forces tearing him apart and resigned to the impossibility of resolving the conflict, Josef K. cannot even commit suicide but must submit to assassination at the hands of the very agency which has frustrated him. It is almost the thought of his degredation, his total failure, which becomes the instrument of execution. The appearance of the double-figure, the Chaplinesque executioners, in this episode is the key to its and the novel's ironic and paradoxical implications.

To insist upon this reading of The Trial as the only pertinent one would be a disservice to the genius of Franz Kafka. In the image of the court he created a verbal key which opens the gate to an approach to many a mystery, not only that of the dichotomous self, even though it may be supposed that this concept was uppermost in his mind. That it is a court of divine justice, as opposed to earthly justice, can be logically concluded. The bureaucracy associated with the court has been chosen as the novel's focal point in other interpretations, in which Josef K. is the anti-hero, caught up, like Chaplin in "Modern Times," in the machinery of an impersonal world. Because of the novel's open symbolism there are occasions for insisting on the viewpoint that Kafka has transcribed a nightmare or has written a case history about a victim of dementia praecox or tuberculosis. In fact, The Trial deserves to be read for what it suggests rather than for what it means; it is Kafka's particular contribution to the novel form that through the manysidedness of his observations he sought to raise, as the novel's substance, the minutiae of life to the level of "the pure, the true, the unalterable" (Journals, p. 534).

The narrative "In the Penal Colony" ("In der Strafkolonie," 1914; published 1919) has a relationship not only to The Trial but also, according to Kafka himself (Letters, p. 149), a somewhat tenuous one to "The Judgment" and a stronger one to "Metamorphosis": Kafka considered publishing the three stories in one volume under the title of Penalties (Strafen). The obvious connection in the latter instance (between the three stories) involves the fact that the three principal figures, Georg Bendemann, Gregor Samsa and the officer in "In the Penal Colony" sentence themselves to death for their inability to function in the "normal" world. Josef K. suffers an at least somewhat similar fate, but it is the structure of the symbolism in both works, The Trial and "In the Penal Colony," which undergirds their kinship. In the stead of the court there is in the novella the authority of the Old Commandant, given tangibility by the execution machine. Replacing Josef K. , there occurs the double-figure of the officer of the execution and the scientific observer (cf. the dog engaged in research, the ape writing a tract for an academy, the doctor probing his wound, the "surveyor" sighting the castle). In these two characters with their antithetical dispositions Kafka once more demonstrates his inner conflict; while the visitor to the penal colony, which is a transparent symbol for the world, for life, refuses to accept the principle, represented by the machine, that guilt characterizes the human condition and punishment must follow, the officer, the Old Commandant's (God's) successor, sacrifices himself to establish the validity of a metaphysical system of accountability. Inevitably in Kafka's work, paradox is present in the climax, since the officer dies in vain; in addition, the story's conclusion, with which Kafka was dissatisfied to the extent that some time later he produced variant endings, portrays the explorer's triumph, his ultimate rejection of the officer's contentions, in a dubious, almost skeptical fashion. Once again, two Kafkas are objectified and given fictitious roles, the one the dutiful son, the other the artist-intellectual; as always the attempt to bridge the gap between the diverse personalities fails—

one is destroyed, one flees in an atmosphere of despair. Because, as was also the case with The Trial, the story acquires a dimension of relevance beyond that of the directly personal, the symbolism of "In the Penal Colony" lends itself to various interpretations. Kafka's disposition to be sadistic, which became evident in The Trial's whipping chamber scene, functions even more pronouncedly in the elaborate description of the machine's operations and reveals its true character to be masochistic. In the light of an identification of the officer with Kafka's bourgeois self, the torment inflicted on him by the machine and the butchering of his body which ensues represent, according to Heinz Politzer, "the tortures to which Kafka, the writer, subjected himself."[7]

Another emphasis which critics have given the story derives from the unmistakably religious connotations implicit in its symbolism; on this level "In the Penal Colony" deals with aspects of the Jewish religion-- its code of laws, the awesome authority of Jehovah-- and the Christian religion--its concept of human guilt and the promise of redemption through death. Climactically, with the slaughter of the officer on the machine and with the scientist's flight from the responsibility of interpreting what he has witnessed, Kafka seems to reject all religious experience as ineffectual.[8] Less cogent than its orientation to religion is the story's tendency to explore through its symbolism the case history of a sexually-founded neurosis (impotency); a list of the details in the story which merge into the substance of a dream to be interpreted by Freudian analysis would be substantial. At any rate, whatever its underlying purpose may be, "In the Penal Colony" constitutes an expertly constructed work of fiction, a story in which narrative force and suspense are sustained by a subtle coordination of mood and symbolism.

The mastery of technique in the short story which Kafka had acquired as the result of a program of writing constantly--sketches, diaries, letters, all became literature -- is exhibited in the collection of prose narratives, some only a page in length, published in 1919 under the title of one of their number: A Country Doctor (Ein Landarzt). The title piece, written in the winter of 1916-1917, demonstrates Kafka's painstakingly developed finesse in presenting his material, for, in essence, the story duplicates the situation described perhaps too impressionistically in "The State of Misery." In both stories Kafka depicts the encounter between the normal self, the ego, and the hidden self, the writer. Where there had been the vaguely defined outline of a protagonist, an "I," there is now the characterization, rich in nuances, of the country doctor, who is Kafka in his ambition to lead the bourgeois life with its social obligations, but who is also modern man in his comprehension of the emptiness of the values to which he clings. Challenging the country doctor, the patient with his mysterious wound appears, once again the child-figure, but no longer a mere ghostly presence. The fleshing out of the country doctor's story, in contrast to the thinness of the depiction of the young man's world, begins with a subtle evocation of the demands his "normal" self makes. First of all, the doctor must fulfill his professional (social) obligations; the ringing of the night-bell sets the story in motion. Almost simultaneously, his personal needs, the desire for love and the urge to procreate, make themselves felt as the doctor's id, the groom, symbolically emerges from the pigsty. Thereupon, Kafka emphasizes the suddenness with which the confrontation with the secret double, the patient, occurs. Having successfully sublimated his sexual drives, the doctor, the ego, imagines himself to be well and finds nothing wrong with the boy he has come to examine. But when he recognizes the patient as a Doppelgänger and takes his place in bed, accepting the boy's wound as his own (the motif of the officer's self-execution in "In the Penal Colony" is repeated here), the tragic nature of his dilemma, his divided self, impresses itself on the doctor as a fatal flaw; he is left in the limbo of the insolubility of his problem, in the misery and conflict of his existence as a writer. At the same time, since Kafka has developed to the utmost his skill in the use of symbols, the country doctor doubles as a representative of the age of science: the moral chaos and social isolation to which a materialistic world has subjected the individual appear with striking clarity in Kafka's portrait of the doctor at the end of the story--dragged naked in the sleigh by runaway horses through the arctic night. Another aspect of "A Country Doctor," calling for attention because of the amount of detail which has relevance, is the background of pathological sexuality--rape, homosexuality, impotence, pederasty, which its nightmarish events and rather hectic (for Kafka) style create. As his letters and journal entries make clear, Kafka was extremely sensitive to the dangers which focussing the spotlight of truth on the self entails. "The devil's work," he once, in a letter to Max Brod, written on July 5, 1922, labeled the creation of literature. "This descent to [the realm of] dark powers," he went on, "this freeing of spirits enchained by nature, [leading to] questionable embraces and to what else may take place down below, of which one is completely unaware, as one writes [one's] stories in the sunlight. Perhaps there is another kind of writing, but I only know this [kind] [...]."

The same elements which comprise the story of the country doctor recur in "A Report to an Academy" ("Ein Bericht für eine Akademie"), one of the longer and more effective pieces in the Country Doctor collection. Sexual perversion is again a hidden motif; here there are sodomy, masochism and scatophilia. The central symbol is, once again, that of the wound, designating the writer, as indeed the story's title itself indicates—a "report." The sophistication of the doubling which marks "A Country Doctor," doctor/patient, is even more pronounced here. The protagonist, an ape who, from Kafka's paradoxical point of view, is the civilized European of the twentieth century, has a counterpart, whom the report surreptitiously identifies. The free animal who the humanized ape has unlearned to be is the protagonist's true self, his creative self, for the talents which he has acquired by imitating human beings--spitting, drinking, fornicating, represent the denigration of self-expression. The schism in the existence of the bureaucrat-writer is, therefore, also in "A Report to an Academy" the starting point for a journey into the regions of despair--sexual, sociological and philosophic, from which, because the crisis cannot be resolved, there is no way out (the very words of the ape's lament).

In its form the embodiment of duality, since it consists of two paragraphs, each of one sentence, "Up in the Gallery" ("Auf der Galerie") illustrates the great skill or, unequivocally, the genius of Kafka as a writer of fiction. In this brief sketch describing the melancholy of a young man in Prague in the years of the First World War, torn between following a call and pursuing a career, Kafka has been able to make a comprehensive statement about the human condition. The protagonist, in a gallery seat at the circus, experiences simultaneously two worlds, a fictitious one, described in the subjunctive mood, and an "actual" one, the world of appearances, described in the indicative. They are opposites in their features and yet the same in the reality of their existence. As the young man acknowledges to himself that, since he embraces both spheres of perception with equal intensity, he has a home in neither, he is filled with despair and hopelessness. His plight is not only that of Kafka, trying to reconcile his need to write (the circus artist is a ready symbol for the artist per se) and his need to fit comfortably into a routine existence, to accommodate himself to "reality," but also the plight of the individual who has suddenly become aware of the duality of the world, half a shadow in the mind, half substance. While the stories in the <u>Country</u> <u>Doctor</u> collection afford insight into both Kafka's personal problems and existential problems in general, his subsequent work involved itself more and more with the ambiguity of the place of the artist in society.

Chapter III - Footnotes

[1] See especially Hellmuth Kaiser: Franz Kafkas Inferno. Reprinted in: Heinz Politzer, ed.: Franz Kafka. Darmstadt 1973.

[2] Franz Kafka: Der Prozess. In: Benno von Wiese, ed.: Der deutsche Roman. Düsseldorf 1963; II, 278.

[3] Cf. "The world of the trial is the complete model of inevitability (<u>Auswegslosigkeit</u>), constructed with all logic, " Beda Allemann: Der deutsche Roman, II, 271.

[4] Die offenen Geheimtüren Franz Kafkas, p. 46.

[5] Die Travestien des Mythos. Bern & München 1963; p. 32.

[6] The Trial and the Theology of Crisis. In Angel Flores, ed.: The Kafka Problem. New York 1946; p. 158 f.

[7] Franz Kafka: Parable and Paradox, p. 104.

[8] See Austin Warren's interpretation in: Cleanth Brooks and Robert Penn Warren, eds.: Understanding Fiction. New York 1943.

CHAPTER IV

Castle and Burrow

Once again, the author who had mastered the technique of the short story and the novella occupied himself with the longer epic form, the novel, and found himself at the same impasse, since, as was the case with One Who Vanished and The Trial, he could not bring himself to consider the work finished. The structure which the dualistic "Up in the Gallery" imposed upon itself and which the tripartite nature of "In the Penal Colony"--exposition, execution, aftermath--made implicit never manifested itself, although The Castle (Das Schloss, written principally in 1922) seems more sequential than The Trial and less disjointed than One Who Vanished. The protagonist, although his name has shrunken from a complete one, i.e., Karl Rossmann, to an abbreviated one, Josef K., to become the mere initial K., has, nevertheless, many more of the attributes of a novelistic portrait. He has no past, but he has a full-blown love affair, and the characters with whom he becomes involved act upon him rather than merely react to him (compare, for example, the figures of Leni and Frieda). The greater cohesiveness of The Castle, which produces its effectiveness as a novel, is reflected in its title that lacks the meandering suggested by (literally) "the process" and the ambiguity of having no title at all. "The castle" identifies both the goal set for the course of the novel and its theme. Interpreters have differed widely as to the precise meaning of the symbol: the female (Neider), a lock (which it is literally), almost a living being (Gray), the citadel of the Self,[1] God (Fürst, p. 27), a labyrinth (Politzer), etc. But a consensus exists as to its basic nature, summarized in Sheppard's comment (p. 41): "The village and the castle are [...] an externalisation of the inner processes of K.'s personality."

As the title indicates, the emphasis in Kafka's consideration of the dichotomy which ruled his life had shifted from the conflict itself to one of the antitheses, which he now set about to explore. At the beginning of the novel K. becomes enmeshed in a fiction since he identifies himself as a surveyor--Gray equates the term with "writer." The German word for surveying, vermessen, has a twofold import; as a verb and the related noun Landmesser it pertains to measuring, as an adjective, however, to measuring out an overabundance for one's self, to being presumptuous. In other words, K. has created a fictitious role of importance for himself. He then insists that the "castle," the only form of authority he is willing to recognize, acknowledge the authenticity of his creation. Even at the outset the castle is only the means by which he hopes to achieve acceptance of what he has authored. In the dualistic fashion which Kafka has adopted as his method of proceeding, the set of values represented by the castle must be balanced by an opposite set of values, which in this instance are clustered around the symbol of the village. This is patently the sum of the circumstances in which K. finds himself at the beginning of the book; the implication that he has come to the village from another life, in which he may have had a wife and family, is made offhandedly and suggests the same sort of inventiveness as that which provided him with a profession, without the seriousness of purpose which characterizes labeling himself a surveyor.

The people who populate the village and the figures who emanate from the castle are the agents of the opposing forces which contend in K.'s mind. The villagers represent a society which does not require a surveyor; it does have need of a school custodian. Although it exhibits a certain reverence for--tolerance of, is perhaps a better phrase-- the mysterious and grand inhabitants of the castle and their Bohemian preoccupations, it properly ignores the significance of the relationship between the two spheres of influence; as a matter of fact, the schoolteacher is too fastidious a man to care to discuss the matter openly. When, in the past, one of the castle emissaries named Sordini had proposed that the village employ a surveyor who might elucidate the meaning of the castle for the village, his plan had been put aside, to be frustrated by neglect. As it happens, Sordini himself would have faded into oblivion for the village, were it not for his "double," that is, his namesake, Sortini, another representative of the castle. Kafka's playfulness in naming his characters seems particularly evident in this instance, in which the similarity of the names exists in strong contrast to the dissimilarity of their connotations and these, in turn, in contrast to the traits which distinguish the one castle official from the other. So it is that the "sordid" one (Sordini) is the model of industriousness, while the select one (Sortini, "sorted out") has made not an intelligent, but an indecent proposal. One Kafka critic has contended that Kafka must have used a dictionary of names in order to produce such convoluted designations.

While the villagers resist every effort made on their behalf to engage
an intermediary who could interpret the influence of the castle on
their lives, the tenants of the castle cannot allow themselves the lux-
ury of being indifferent to the situation. They do, after all, present
themselves to the populace now and then. These occasions attract the
presence of the women of the village in particular, who keep their
relationship to the castle hierarchy strictly sexual (except for one
of their number). In the person of K. the castle is confronted by
someone who does not offer submission or disregard, but a challenge. The contact between the village and the castle is for him the
instrumentality by which he can be catapulted to the heights of the
castle. K.'s progress in achieving recognition from the castle is
rather slow, but steady; it follows the course of Kafka's success
as a writer. As the story begins, the contradictory import of two
telephone calls nevertheless produces a first breach in the castle
walls; K.'s right to be noticed by the officials is acknowledged. And
soon two castle functionaries appear, Artur and Jeremias, for the
purpose of offering the surveyor their assistance. K. has boasted
of the availability of his assistants, but Artur and Jeremias are sup-
posedly not these. K.'s first impression is that they are twins, and
in that capacity they join or even bring to a climax a series of twin
figures in the Kafka canon, the celluloid balls and assistants in
"Blumfeld, an Elderly Bachelor" ("Blumfeld, ein älterer Junggesell"), the warders in The Trial, the boarders (although they are
triplets) in "Metamorphosis," the vagabonds in One Who Vanished,
among others. The origin of Kafka's use of the literary device of
the double may be related to an incident early in his career as a
writer which he described in a letter to Max Brod from Prague, on
October 13, 1912: "Two figures, which were supposed to appear (in
One Who Vanished) I suppressed. [But] through the whole time, during which I was writing, they came running up behind me, and since
in the novel itself they were supposed to be raising their arms and
making a fist, they did exactly that to me. They were, at any rate,
livelier than that which I was writing." Following this account in the
letter, there appears the statement which is fundamental to an understanding of Kafka's work; Kafka confesses: "I am my novel, I am
my stories." Artur and Jeremias, about whose significance there are
as many conjectures as there are about the identity of the castle,
constitute, in their function as a literary device, Kafka's abilities,
his talent as a writer. Subsequently, they go their separate ways:
they become two people, one who is soon enmeshed in the life of the
village, with K.'s abandoned mistress as his companion (Jeremias),

the other who returns to the celibacy of the castle (Artur). In this way they change from symbolic figures, with general applicability, to mythic ones, pertaining to the schizophrenic propensity of the modern psyche, as it is evoked in the tortured self-analysis of Franz Kafka.

The castle next makes another overture to the self-appointed surveyor. A messenger from a castle plenipotentiary Klamm finds his way to K. with a letter of praise. The sophistication of the metaphoric writing in which Kafka engages in depicting this course of events indicates the shift in focus which characterizes The Castle and distinguishes it from Kafka's previous work: Kafka's involvement with the Dichter-figure per se becomes evident. The young man who brings K. Klamm's seal of approval is Barnabas, "son of the father." In K.'s eyes Barnabas resembles the assistants.[2] For Walter Sokel Barnabas represents K.'s "pure" self, his writer-self. Because the relationship between Barnabas and Klamm is a tenuous, although vital one, it duplicates that which immediately evolves between K. and Klamm. The similarity between the names Kafka and Klamm cannot be coincidental. Before too long, K. is able to see Klamm through a peephole, that is, in his mind's eye. K. perceives Klamm to be a man with glasses, seated at a desk, for the moment resting his eyes. This portrait of the writer, the model for whom could have been Flaubert, has a duplicate in a description which appears among Kafka's "fragments": "I was a guest among the dead . . . ," Kafka begins his entry. "A desk stood a little apart so that I did not notice it immediately; behind it sat a man with a heavy body."[3] The overlapping symbolism in the three figures, the tormented writer in hell, the wearied man behind the peephole, the aspiring messenger conveying communications, the content of which is fictitious, depicts various aspects--almost: age, maturity and youth, of the writer-figure who Kafka had become, now that his affliction, tuberculosis, had decreed the end of his exploring other avenues of self-fulfillment.

The failure of any effort on K.'s part to pursue a way of life independent of the castle is established by the course of his relationship with Frieda, the barmaid whom he meets during his search for Klamm. The choice of the name Frieda,[4] "peace," must have been deliberate in the light of Kafka's relentless striving for ironic effect. Whether or not the character Kafka created for The Castle is modeled on Milena Jesenska, as Brod insists, Frieda's function in the novel is, according to critical consensus (for which Emrich provided the impetus), to involve K. in a genuine love affair with a woman. K.'s excursion into intimacy and domesticity is brief and disastrous. As happened to an appreciable extent in actuality, K.'s (thus Kafka's) first love affair was doomed because his faithfulness was in doubt from the very beginning, called into question by his passion for literature. Frieda attracts K. because she professes to be Klamm's mistress, perhaps his inspiration, his muse. Possessing her, K. finds himself not elevated to Parnassian heights, but on the floor among pools of stale beer. When Frieda transforms his garret room into a comfortable, liveable place, K. becomes suspicious of her and resentful of his assistants, who, under her guidance, have joined the couple to constitute a "family." Kafka's sometime hope of combining breadwinning and writing seems to be symbolically represented in this arrangement.

Like the embodiment of K.'s conscience, the landlady Gardena comes opportunely into the picture and rebukes K. for the travesty he has made of his life. As her name implies, she symbolizes Kafka's favorite myth, the story of man's fall and his expulsion from the garden; Gardena herself lives in exile as Klamm's cast-off mistress. In this guise, she is also Frieda's conscience to such an extent that she almost appears to be her mother. Ridiculed by Gardena for his presumption in aspiring to be on an equal footing with Klamm, K. is so much the more impelled to find his way back to Klamm. Already imminent at this point is K.'s decision to renounce his share of the domestic haven which Frieda has established for him. As K. regrets the confusion in the matter of goals which has resulted from his relationship with Frieda, so Kafka exposes in one of his aphorisms his awareness of his own lack of perspicacity in refusing obstinately to devote himself to writing: he speaks of man's being driven from the garden (and into a sexual encounter) as a fiction, since man may still be in the garden under the burden of not knowing that he is there. Having left Frieda and venturing into the "Inn of the Masters" (Herrenhof), K. experiences, while waiting in the inn's courtyard for Klamm, a moment of ecstasy, which his sexual union with Frieda has not provided.

The nightmare of a life of domestic tranquility comes upon K. when he assumes the role of school custodian and provider for himself and his "family." On the first occasion that presents itself K. escapes from the shambles of his household and takes refuge in the home of Barnabas, the messenger, in whom he feels that, despite appearances, his hope for the future lies. In the absence of Barnabas, K.'s

involvement with his sisters, which now becomes Kafka's preoccupation
in the novel, recapitulates Kafka's analysis of his dichotomous situation. In essence, Olga and Amalia are two aspects of one person: the
motive force in Olga's life is her concern for her sister; Amalia has
borrowed to wear on the most momentous occasion of her life the neck-
lace which belongs to and, in a sense, identifies her sister. Their
names (cf. Weinberg and Gray), one meaning work and the other
holiness, apply not to themselves, but to their vis-à-vis. And the
story of Amalia's "fall," told and interpreted, it should be noted, by
Olga, gives expression to the same pain which K. experiences as an
outsider who can neither reconcile himself to his loneliness nor
mitigate it. This lengthy novella about Amalia provides a restatement
of the theme of The Castle and thus parallels the chaplain's sermon
in The Trial and Therese's narrative in One Who Vanished. In common with the figures of the man from the country and the door-
keeper and, as Kafka himself has demonstrated, Georg Bendemann
and his friend in Russia, Amalia and her reptilian tempter Sortini
have the purpose of establishing a relationship, of revealing an attitude. Amalia, in her encounter with the castle official who tests
the strength of her resolve by offering her an easy alternative, the
common destiny of the village women, reenacts K.'s being confronted by the opposites of the castle and the village, and her re-
fusal to submit foreshadows the life of the pariah which will be K.'s
lot when he chooses, as he must, to make his siege of the castle
his exclusive concern. As Kafka indicates simultaneously by separating the doubles Artur and Jeremias, K. must make a decision
about rejoining Frieda, who has had to content herself with his sub-
stitute Jeremias, or passing her by and following Artur back to the
castle; in the Amalia episode the same circumstances pertain: K.
must either sympathize with Amalia and act on her example or accept the compromise which Olga has effected: respect for Amalia's
position but a life divorced from it. K. duplicates Kafka's feat in
pursuing a literary career at the expense of relinquishing the "normal" satisfactions of life and of dispensing with recognition and the
assurance that comes with a sense of self-fulfillment.

The dubious rewards of the celibate life, of the pursuit of Dichtertum,
become evident when K. makes his way to the Inn of the Masters subsequent to his initiation into the mysteries of Amalia's fate. He has
been told that the castle has made a further commitment in the case
of the surveyor: a high castle dignitary, Erlanger (erlangen means
to attain), has condescended to interview K. Instead of receiving this

72

tentative kind of a nod of recognition from the castle, K. stumbles
into a room at the inn in which an even more highly placed surrogate
for the count of the castle, named Westwest in the most naive form of
doubling, waits. It is Bürgel; the connotation of the name is that he is
a "guarantor." He provides K. with the key to the innermost castle
door, behind which the secret of the castle's power of attraction lies
revealed. As Bürgel, who has retired to his bed, explains to the strife-
worn contender at his side, acceptance into the company of the table
round, the castle elite, the circle of immortals in literature, cannot
be obtained through effort and dedication alone, but occurs by chance,
in a random fashion which is the height of irony. To compound the
bitterness in his formula for literary success, Kafka depicts K. as
asleep when he is presented with this guarantee. Furthermore, he is
dreaming of his victory in a struggle with a "god," but at the last
moment the "god" turns out to be a giggling girl. When K. emerges
from Bürgel's room, he may be either inside the castle or in the
hallway of the inn. The description of the activities of the castle
functionaries at this point is more appropriate to the nature of their
"work" than to a night of relaxation at an inn; they are buried in
protocol--in manuscripts. Even K.'s papers are there. Has his
fondest hope, literary achievement, admittance to the castle, been
realized?

But Kafka will not allow fiction to persevere over reality; his protagonist, despite the insight which his creator has gained, continues
his struggle for enlightenment, enticed by a second Frieda, named
Pepi (a nickname for Josef, K.'s first name), who wishes to lure him
into a shadowy repose, and, at the same time, challenged by the landlady of the Inn of the Masters, who promises a change of clothes, a
change of perspective. The lack of resolution on K.'s part in The
Castle's final scene reiterates the theme of duality which pervades
the novel, in the basic dichotomy of castle and village, in the duplication of characters (Jeremias-Artur, Olga-Amalia, [5] Sortini-Sor-
dini), and in the conflicting goals, symbolized by the protagonist's
guises as surveyor and school custodian. Since Kafka never writes
an allegory, as Brod has correctly contended, the ambiguity of the
events and characters in The Castle does not lend itself to having
just one explanation. K.'s dilemma is not that of the writer alone.
The interpretations of the novel by Brod and Gray, which coincide
in equating K.'s quest with a search for grace are pertinent in that
Kafka's compounding of art and religion (cf. his definition of writing
as a form of prayer, Wedding Preparations, p. 348) affords a struc-

ture for his fiction. In turn, the protagonist as a seeker for God and God's grace converts readily into an existentialistic non-hero, when accordingly the castle loses its significance as the seat of divinity and becomes a chimera, the symbol of meaninglessness; from this perspective Philippi and Emrich, for example, write their interpretations. In all probability the fascination which Kafka's work has for most readers comes from his skilfull depiction of man in his perplexity, driven to look for meaning in his life and yet restricted to leading a life of empty routine. The fact that the writer, the Dichter, in modern times takes upon himself the task of analyzing his own tormented self as it represents every man's remains concealed behind the mask of fiction. In a study of the purport of modern literature, Charles Glicksberg has established this principle and has, indirectly, summarized the plot of The Castle: "The self, if it can be represented at all must be pictured as forever changing, a consciousness beset with inescapable contradictions, a consciousness of something outside that remains uncognizable."[6]

In Kafka's last stories, a collection of which was published in 1924 with the title of A Hunger-Artist (Ein Hungerkünstler), the conflict, the outward manifestation of which has been the double, has been almost completely internalized. Kafka, having removed himself from the arena in which the Bohemian writer and the bourgeois engage in combat, focuses his attention on the artist's inner self. In Politzer's words (Franz Kafka: Parable and Paradox, p. 302), "now [his protagonists] resemble Kafka the writer rather than Kafka the metaphysical outcast." The title of the story "A Hunger-Artist" announces its chief concern: it describes the divergence between the body and mind, between the human being and the artist. In portraying the artist whose talent is fasting, Kafka divides himself into a physical self and a spiritual self; the latter gains the ascendency over the former. But the final victory belongs to the body, as the motif of the panther's taking over the hunger-artist's cage makes clear, since in overcoming its physical presence, the spirit negates itself; the mind, Geist, goes out of existence together with the flesh, Leben. In treating this theme, Kafka joined the company of Thomas Mann and Hermann Hesse, as well as many lesser-known German authors of the early twentieth century. Roy Pascal has pointed out the particular significance "Geist" had for them in their epigonal idealism: "[Geist] embraced more than mind and intellect, emphatically more than science and learning, and affirmed a pledge to positive 'spiritual' values and goals."[7] This kind of genuflection at the altar of

74

Dichtertum marks the attitude of the protagonist in "First Sorrow" ("Erstes Leid"), the trapeze artist, who has become so absorbed in his art that normal activity has become impossible for him. He breaks into tears at the realization of his incapacity both to achieve perfection in his gymnastics (that is, for Kafka, mental gymnastics) and to continue a relationship with the everyday world. His despair duplicates that of the young man in "Up in the Gallery," but in the latter instance, the protagonist is analytical, while in "First Sorrow" he is immersed in hopelessness: he has come down from the gallery and has taken the place of the equestrian.

In this final phase of his concern with the fragmentation of the personality, particularly that of the Dichter, Kafka has lost interest in an actual representation of the inner conflict; he concentrates instead on the sense of the doubling which the writer experiences. Thus, in "A Little Woman" ("Eine kleine Frau"), the emphasis is not placed on this antagonist of the story's principal figure as a projection of his self, namely as a personification of his craftsmanship. Although Fürst calls the little woman the poetic muse, "Frau Kunst," and she aptly symbolizes the demands that Kafka makes on himself as a writer and the relentlessness of his dissatisfaction with his own work, Kafka describes the relationship between the little woman and the "I" of the story for its own sake, as a relationship which has an intrinsic meaning. The impossibility of a resolution of the Dichter's dilemma, the durability of the conflict, which will last, as may be presumed from "The Hunter Gracchus" ("Der Jäger Gracchus"), even beyond the grave, is the content of "A Little Woman." An elaboration of the study of the warring factions within the writer occurs in "The Singer Josefine" ("Josefine, die Sängerin"); here not only Josefine's own ambiguity about her talent but also that of her audience come under scrutiny. The choice of the name is Kafka's signature, together with the transmogrification into an animal, which also happens in "A Hunger-Artist" itself. The mutual dependency which exists between an artist and his public serves Kafka well as material on which he may sharpen his sense of irony. Like the inhabitants of the village who would concede that the castle has no useful purpose in their lives, although they subject themselves to its authority, vested in its venal officials, the nation of mice in the story relies on one of its number who will enact the role of martyr in a pageant, the meaning of which has been lost. The mice comprehend Josefine's art as little as she has confidence in its efficacy. Nevertheless, as Kafka concluded in his letter of July 5, 1922, to Max Brod, defining the writer, he must be a scapegoat and subject himself to the torment of probing the depths of his being so that the rest of humanity need know this kind of suffering only vicariously.

Several of Kafka's posthumously published stories attest to his continuing preoccupation with the artist's self-doubt. "A Hybrid" ("Eine Kreuzung") is one of the most transparent pieces on the subject by Kafka; his writer-self appears in the customary guise of an animal, a cross between a cat and a lamb. The predatory cat signifies that part of Kafka, the _Dichter_, which seeks to encompass all, to absorb within itself the total being, of which it is one aspect. The lamb obviously symbolizes the sacrificial element in the artist's personality, the willingness to be consumed, used up in the process of writing. The story's unique component is the delineation of the viewpoint of the pet's keeper; like the ego, confronted by the id, or the rational human being, confronted by the irrationality of the poetic gift, he longs to be able to ignore the beast and to let it die. Having much the same vantage point, but written with greater sophistication, "The Giant Mole" ("Der Riesenmaulwurf"), which Brod ascribes to the work of the post-war years, presents another portrait of the artist as a grotesque creature. In this narrative, however, the observing self or ego is split into the characters of the discoverer of the mole, a schoolteacher, and the "merchant" who seeks him out. Both have become writers despite themselves, that is, despite their prosaic occupations, because of the fascination which the mole, whose existence they both aver and doubt, has for them. Their distrust of one another in regard to establishing the authenticity of the beast's presence expresses, once again, Kafka's suspicion that his talent as a writer might be the product of phantasy: as a rational being, he debates the issue with himself; ironically, both sides present arguments which undermine their own validity.

Of the two last stories which Kafka wrote, "The Research Project of a Dog" ("Forschungen eines Hundes") and "The Structure" ("Der Bau"), it is not certain which came first; for their part, Heller and Beug have given Summer, 1922, as the date for "The Research Project" and Winter, 1923, as that for "The Structure." By critical consensus, however, both deal with the writer and his work. In the document by the canine investigator, which necessarily bears a resemblance to the ape's report to an academy, there is a double perspective. Initially, the author distinguishes himself from other dogs and describes the process of his estrangement. He then analyzes the

elitism, of which he finds himself to be a part. In considering what
has turned him into a researcher, that is, a writer, the protagonist
theorizes that his questioning of the obvious, the fact that the race of
dogs perseveres, is sustained, has segregated him from the pack.
The posing of the existentialist dilemma would seem, according to
this speculation, to be the point at which the artist breaks with society, which is never puzzled about the source of the power which maintains it. For the investigating dog, a specific instance marks the occasion of his initiation as an outsider. He once observes seven acrobatic dogs who elicit music out of the air through their art. At this
point the curious onlooker becomes aware both of the nature of dogs
and of the musicians' contravention of this nature: "These dogs here
were in violation of the law."[8] In this wise Kafka makes the exclusion
of the artist the justification for his existence. Kafka then proceeds,
with some redundancy, to explore the character of the artist, in actuality, that of the writer. To this end he invents the breed of the
aerial dog (Lufthunde) and asks himself the question (p. 261): "What
purpose does their profession have?" Their peculiarity, so the protagonist concludes, must serve to define what is ordinary. This
theory enables the dog to proceed with his outlandish way of life,
his exclusivity and his probing of the sense of existence. Kafka's
ruminations about himself as a writer have no ending.

The most patent and likewise most potent appraisal of the fate of
being a writer ever made by Kafka is afforded by "The Structure."
The metaphor for the Dichter in this case, presumably closing out
a list of astonishing variety, from the repulsive insect to the aerial
dog, is sheer animal consciousness. This animality has established
a vast system of defenses within which it maintains itself; that this
"burrow" is Kafka's literary work is critical dogma (see, for instance, Politzer and Bridgwater). In describing the torturous passage-
ways the beast has constructed, Kafka parodies both his convoluted
style and the intricacy of his thought. In the final analysis, the story
proposes that the ego, the conscious self, has become immaterial
in that it exists merely as an awareness of the burrow it has built,
the work it has created, which alone has a physical presence. Politzer
concludes that, at last, Kafka has entered the castle and has found
it to be his grave. The assumption is that the individual Kafka, who
once had vied with the Dichter image, has ceased to be. In the bitterest of ironies, it develops in "The Structure" that the beast's arrangement of labyrinths, which has absorbed the identity of its ar-
chitect, is itself threatened with destruction. Kafka seems to fear

that with the death of his person the edifice he has constructed will collapse, as if only the integrity of the living artist were able to validate his work. In Günther Anders' book on Kafka the conclusion is drawn from this kind of relationship between the writer and his creation that Kafka would consequently have wanted his manuscripts destroyed: "It is because his writing possessed ... only artistic perfection that he considered it suspect and therefore ordered it to be destroyed," Anders suggests. [9] Thus "The Structure" ends on an ominous note, with the animal self (the writer) thoroughly transformed into a fiction, awaiting an attack from "without," from death or the necessity for the destruction of his magnificent labyrinths, an auto de fe. In this ultimate dichotomy, the palpable existence of the work of art and the impossibility of the existence of the work of art, [10] the series of doubles, beginning with very tangible opposing selves, proceeding toward the epitome of abstraction, comes to an end.

Chapter IV - Footnotes

[1] Patrick Bridgwater: Kafka and Nietzsche. Bonn 1974; p. 90. Further: "[The castle] has no objective existence."

[2] Franz Kafka: Das Schloss. New York 1946; p. 34.

[3] Hochzeitsvorbereitungen auf dem Lande, p. 259.

[4] The curious fact that most of the women characters in Kafka's works have names ending in "a" (Klara, Magdalena, i.e., Leni, Anna, Olga, Amalia, Gardena, Brunelda) points to the generic concept which he had of women: they are not to be readily distinguished one from the other. At the same time, it can only be coincidental that the women who were actually important in his life--his sister Ottla, his first mistress Milena, the "wife" of his last year Dora, also had names ending in "a."

[5] According to Emrich, Amalia's opposite is Frieda.

[6] The Self in Modern Literature. University Park, Pa., 1963; p. xii.

[7] From Naturalism to Expressionism. New York 1973; p. 297.

[8] Franz Kafka: Beschreibung eines Kampfes. New York 1946; p. 247.

[9] A. Steer and A.K. Thorlby, trans.: Franz Kafka. New York 1960; p. 95.

[10] See Thorlby, p. 98: "Kafka's writing is directed against the absurdity not of the world, but of writing"; and Bridgwater, p. 149: "[Kafka] argues that [...] the highest form of art [is] silence"; also Hall and Lind, p. 75: "Kafka appears to have regarded the corpus of his writings as he did his body--something to be annihilated."

CHAPTER V

The Use and Abuse of the Double

It is an inescapable fact that Kafka regarded literature as a vehicle
for self-examination. In his work excursions into prophecy and social
criticism were incidental. The truths which he sought to establish came
not from statistics but from hidden depths of the self. His definition of
the writer centered around the concept of the scapegoat, who, in the
terms of Hall and Lind's study of Kafka (p. 56), succeeds "in bringing
into the preconscious where it is available much of what remains ir-
retrievably unconscious for most people." These unknown regions,
thus brought to light, reveal themselves to be both the source of conflict in the individual and the scene of continuing warfare since the
inner self is perceived by the observing self to be, literally, its opposite. The consequence is that, according to Robert Rogers, "when
an author wishes to depict mental conflict within a single mind a most
natural way for him to dramatize it is to represent the mind by two or
more characters. Such a technique is a natural one whether the author
is aware of what he is doing or not."[1] Kafka could hardly have avoided
using the literary device of the double because of the intensity of his
speculations about the nature of individual existence and his sensitivity to the dichotomies he found in himself.

Whether or not the frequent appearance of the double in his work
represents the deliberate employment of a kind of symbolism--at
least occasionally the doubling is unequivocal, Kafka was not bound
by convention in this aspect of his writing. Only in the sense that he
was impelled to give his findings in the exploration of the self the form
of fiction, to narrate them in the guise of past event and a diversity of
characters does he acknowledge literary tradition. Nevertheless, his
intimate acquaintance with a great deal of literature, particularly that
in the category of the masterpiece--critically acclaimed work, cannot have been without influence on the development of his craftsmanship. His familiarity with the novels of Jean Paul, the inventor of the
label "Doppelgänger" and, as his work testifies, an ardent advocate
of the effectiveness of the device of doubling, points to an awareness
on Kafka's part of the basic concept, that of two lookalikes, usually
twins, who complement one another, while exhibiting contrasting
characters, like positive and negative electrical poles. The literary

use of the double became more sophisticated in the stories of E. T. A. Hoffmann, certainly a precursor of Kafka; here, the person of the artist is rent into a rational part, usually the embodiment of conscience and an irrational part, a cauldron of wild desires and also creative impulses. In his fondness for French literature, in particular for Flaubert, on whose life he sometimes thought to model his own, Kafka would have found in his reading instances of dédoublement, "the phenomenon, often vividly hallucinatory, of a person's being aware of the presence of another self, acting independently of one's accustomed self."[2] Another appearance of the double, in one of the most eminent cases in world literature, occurs in Dostoevsky's "The Double," which, it may be assumed, Kafka knew. The two identities of the protagonist in this story produce the effect of dédoublement and also follow the pattern established by Hoffmann. The supposition that Kafka read in translation the stories of Poe and Stevenson in which double-figures occur must be left a matter of conjecture. There is no doubt, however, about Kafka's enchantment with the Yiddish theater and, on one occasion, with the performance of a play in which a man and wife, identically dressed, represented the chorus; under these circumstances, according to H. Platzer Collins, "the ambivalent sex sometimes implicit in [Kafka's] double-figure had its foundation."[3]

Although Kafka's reading would have informed him that there are two (indeed) basic types of doubling, one spatial, called autoscopy, and one temporal, called multiple personality--"behavioral dissociation in time,"[4] his use of the double does not indicate an attempt to distinguish between the two categories; so, for example, Artur and Jeremias are physically doubles, while in the same work K. and Barnabas are different aspects, dissociations, of the same individual. It is the latter type of doubling which is truly ubiquitous in Kafka. The frequency with which both kinds of double appear in his work arouses the suspicion that Kafka found this literary device apt for the depiction of an inner distress which he regarded as fundamental in his character. In a study of Kafka's "problem," which he may not have perceived to be homosexuality, Ruth Tiefenbrun, who makes such an assumption, concludes: "The technique of separating the different aspects of the self and thinking of them as completely different individuals is characteristic of certain types of disturbed individuals. Kafka depicts his divided self consistently in a great number of his narratives."[5] A less simplistic interpretation of Kafka's employment of autoscopy and dissociation seems pertinent.

The complexity of the situation which is delineated in literature through the agency of the double has been described by Rogers in his psychoanalytic study of the device. Defects in personality structure, he makes clear (p. 16 f.), "may be said to develop between love and hate; heterosexuality and homosexuality; ego libido and object libido; the Eriksonian categories of autonomy and dependence: mas- ochism and sadism; activity and passivity. Fissures may also be said to appear between the psychic constellations of id, ego, and superego, or between the oral, anal, and phallic stages of libidinal development [...]." Virtually all of these manifestations of neurosis appear in Kafka's personality and are reflected in his work. The love-hate relationship between Kafka and his father or, actually, his parents is, without doubt, the salient feature in his early stories, while its aftermath remains an important element in the rest of his work. Thus, reverence for and fear of the father motivate the dissociation of Georg Bendemann into super-ego self (conscience) and id-self (rebelliousness); the ensuing conflict necessitates the destruction of the total personality. Another instance of the ambiguity of feelings toward the father or parents follows immediately in the novel One Who Vanished; here Pollunder and Green represent the loving father and the devious, hateful one or, as one critic surmises, both mother and father, toward whom Karl, mirroring Kafka himself, evinces ambiv- alent emotions. In one of his last narratives, Kafka, writing about K., depicts a place, the castle, as a person with some of the features of the father in earlier stories; here the symbol itself is a double, on the one hand, something yearned for; on the other, something for- bidding.

Insofar as the doubling in the Kafka canon may indicate an uncertainty in his orientation to heterosexuality, if not a commitment to homosexu- ality, the stories afford ample evidence. In a study of Kafka's dreams, as he revealed them in his journals, letters and sketches, two (a signif- icant number?) researchers attest to the fact that Kafka's dreaming exhibited "ambivalence toward men and toward women [and] the mas- culinized woman" (Hall and Lind, p. 36). It is obvious that there are no sympathetic women characters in Kafka; although Emrich has writ- ten a brief in behalf of Frieda, his case is weak. Kafka's inability to develop a positive attitude toward women is best illustrated by the oblique case of doubling which occurs in The Trial. The characters concerned are Elsa and Erna (actually the name of Felice's sister); the former, constituting an allusion to a Wagnerian virgin, is a pros- titute, the latter, a saintly little girl. Both are a necessary and yet at the same time peripheral part of Josef K.'s life. Perhaps the most telling instance of Kafka's sexual disorientation is autobiographical; in a letter to Max Brod (Letters, p. 82) he writes of an illness which had brought him to the doctor's office. Here he fainted (fainting is another form of the sleep to which many a Kafka character falls victim); as he lay on the doctor's couch, so Kafka reveals: "I felt myself to be so much a girl that I sought to smooth my skirt with my fingers." There were two Kafkas on that occasion. A feminine counterpart perseveres in his life as reflected in his writing, since the girl who has the nickname for "Josef," Pepi, appears in the pages of The Castle and tries to lure K. into her sphere of influence and since one of his last characterizations of the artist and himself is Josefine.

A theory about the nature of doubling, held both generally and specifically by Stekel, [6] the psychologist in whom Kafka was interested, states that self-love is the root of the phenomenon; narcissism, logically, is the progenitor of the mirror-image. Evidence of Kafka's preoccupation with himself is legion. Is there any critic who does not regard his characters as projections or dissociations of the self that Kafka created for his fiction? [7] A significant aspect of the rapt attention with which Kafka regarded himself involves the sense of repugnance which his own body aroused in him and, somewhat relatedly, the fascination which clothing had for him. Hall and Lind in their analysis of the dream material in Kafka reach the conclusion (p. 91) that "rejection of his body resulted in neurasthenia and hypochondria and was one of the reasons for becoming consumptive." Of course, Kafka's dislike of his body, while seeming to be the reverse of narcissism, actually attests to the importance he attached to his physical self, which he was inspired to describe at every turn with an amazing variety of metaphors, most of them animalistic. Clothing, about which Kafka was particular in that he exhibited an extremely conservative taste, as if his manner of dressing himself would serve to obliterate his presence, occurs as a topic of mutual concern for K. and the landlady of the Inn of the Masters, who is thereby contrasted with the other landlady in The Castle, who has no sympathy for K.

The masochistic element in Kafka's metamorphosis of his body into vermin, a hybrid, an ape, a corpse, a useless and grotesque object (Odradek), a dog, etc., is even more pronounced in other features of his work. The whipping of Franz and Willem in The Trial is an instance of self-flagelation. In the penal colony the tortures of the execution machine expunge the guilt of the flesh. Together with this perverted pleasure in a denigration of the self, there exists in Kafka and his work its twin, a perverted pleasure in the pain of others. The father's attack on his insect-son, the wounds from which lead to Gregor's death, has overtones of a homosexual rape. The misery of Karl Rossmann's life, while he is in bondage to Brunelda, duplicates, to a degree, that which Kafka experienced as a boy at the hands of his father: locked out on a balcony, having been ejected from the warmth of the parental bed. K.'s cruelty to his "assistants" repeats the pattern, which is immediately taken up again by Gisa's abusive treatment of K. These aberrations which underlie some of the events in Kafka's narratives coincide with imagery which derives, in all likelihood, from the contortions of Kafka's psychological development. He had a preference for anal contexts, perhaps as the result of a castration complex (see Neider; Lind and Hall). The insect Gregor is attacked from behind, and his "back" bleeds. The execution machine's victim lies face down, and needles bloody his back. Frequently, the posture of a character is that of moving about on his hands and knees like a dog, as Block does, for example. The protagonist in "The Research Project of a Dog" is dismayed at the sight of the acrobatic dogs who walk on two feet and consequently expose themselves.

It would be impossible to ascertain if Kafka was aware of these ramifications of the double symbol in literature. Too much scholarly effort has already been devoted to an attempt to establish Kafka as a philosopher--the disciple of Kierkegaard; as a sociologist--the champion of oppressed minorities and the Malthus of the course of Fascism; and as a philologist--the self-taught professor of historical linguistics, so that to put forth the thesis that Kafka was a student of the use of literary devices in the novel and of the Doppelgänger motif in particular would be merely to compound the mischief. Kafka's involvement with the double as metaphor must have come about as a natural occurrence, a logical step in the process of his becoming an author. In Kafka's case experimentation with the double-figure would have been a more than likely procedure, since the material he sought to fashion into fiction and the experience which formed it both were innately liable to find expression in terms of doubling.

Chapter V - Footnotes

[1] The Double in Literature. Detroit 1970; p. 29.

[2] Conveniently defined in: Michel Carrouges: Kafka versus Kafka (trans. Emmett Parker). University, Alabama, 1968; p. 47 (translator's note).

[3] "Kafka's 'Double-Figure' as a Literary Device," p. 107.

[4] Rogers, p. 15.

[5] Moment of Torment. Carbondale & Edwardsville 1973; p. 59.

[6] See Ralph Tymms: Doubles in Literary Psychology. Cambridge 1949; p. 41.

[7] See Glicksberg, although he does not refer specifically to Kafka, p. xiv: "Whatever mask the writer may assume, in his writings he is presenting in effect a symbolic version of himself in different disguises, though this version represents a 'second self' rather than a strictly autobiographical self."

CONCLUSIONS

The object of Kafka criticism is not to replace Kafka's work; in other words, the ambiguity which exists there in a recreation of the many-sidedness of life itself must remain its salient feature. However, the very act of translating the truism that life is full of uncertainties[1] into literature in the form of fiction presupposes that a continuation of the search for meaning, the attempt to explore the ambiguities which the author has initiated, will follow. This study of one aspect of the Kafka canon, the preponderance of doubles, has endeavored to add to the significance already present in his stories by describing and analyzing one of the means Kafka used to construct his fictitious world mirroring the real one. The symbol of the double Kafka found in his own nature; its relevance to an understanding of Kafka's personality is therefore apparent. Even more pertinent is the functioning in Kafka's fiction of this literary device for establishing the dichotomy in the self, since Kafka the writer was the ultimate victor over Kafka the man.

The depiction of man's schizophrenic state in a world devoid of any kind of unity or harmony, which Kafka's stories afford, have made him the most representative author in twentieth century literature. In this context, Hermann Pongs evaluates Kafka's achievement highly and sees in his protagonists the prototype of modern man, "the individual called 'they' (der Mensch des 'man'), without true identity, the one who lives without light, seasick on solid ground, ambivalent [in being placed] between instincts and ambitions, exposed to the uncertainties of values."[2]

Along with its function as the symbol of ambivalence, the double serves as a representative of ambiguity, another trenchant aspect of contemporary life. In the tragic situation of a valueless world, Kafka's doubles, like the arresting officers and Josef K.'s executioners, are also ridiculous. The comic effect of the three boarders in "Metamorphosis," of the three bank clerks in The Trial, of Blumfeld's two assistants, etc., like figures in a Chaplin movie, provide Kafka's sober accounts of the misfortunes of his anti-heroes with the dimension of satire. The irony in Kafka's writing which these triplets and doubles underscore suggests the principle which Northrop Frye has put forward that realism in literature tends to become satire and thereby to produce allegory and myth. This study may serve as the beginning of an investigation of that proposition in regard to Kafka's work. Then there are other metaphors besides that of the double which Kafka employed with some frequency--clothing and names, for example, which lend themselves to the kind of analysis undertaken here. On the whole, it is the study of Kafka's fiction as fiction, an interpretation of the Kafka canon which recent criticism has just entered upon, which provides fresh prospects for the continuing pursuit of meaning in Kafka. One critic, even while affording enlightenment about Kafka's work, has issued a word of caution: "We do not know, for Kafka did not know either."[3] Paradoxically, for that reason, because he did not know, Kafka wrote his works and critics comment on them.

Conclusions - Footnotes

[1] It has been contended that Kafka's stories are logical extensions of commonly accepted metaphors: "to die like a dog" supplies the final chapter for The Trial; to be considered "lower than vermin" instigates the "Metamorphosis," etc.

[2] Franz Kafka, Dichter des Labyrinths. Heidelberg 1960; p. 40.

[3] Politzer: Franz Kafka: Parable and Paradox; p. 217.

SELECT BIBLIOGRAPHY

Primary Sources

The edition is that of the <u>Gesammelte</u> <u>Werke</u> published by Schocken
Books, unless otherwise noted.

Kafka, Franz: Amerika. New York 1953.
Beschreibung eines Kampfes. New York 1946.
Briefe (1902-1924). New York 1958.
Briefe an Felice und andere Korrespondenz,
Erich Heller & Joachim Zeug ed. Frankfurt
1967 (Fischer).
Briefe an Milena. New York 1952.
Erzählungen und kleine Prosa. New York 1946.
Hochzeitsvorbereitungen auf dem Lande. New
York 1953.
Der Prozess. New York 1958.
Das Schloss. New York 1946.
Tagebücher 1910-1923. Frankfurt 1954
(Fischer).

Secondary Sources

Albérès, R. M. & Pierre DeBoisdeffre: Kafka: The Torment of Man, trans. Wade Baskin, New York 1968.

Anders, Günther: Franz Kafka, trans. A. Steer & A. K. Thorlby. New York 1960.

Beissner, Friedrich: Der Erzähler Franz Kafka. Stuttgart 1952.

Bridgwater, Patrick: Kafka and Nietzsche. Bonn 1974.

Brod, Max: Franz Kafka. Frankfurt 1962.

Canetti, Elias: Der andere Prozess. München 1969.

Carrouges, Michel: Kafka versus Kafka. University, Alabama 1968.

Collins, H. Platzer: Kafka's "Double-Figure" as a Literary Device. Monatshefte 55 (Jan. 1963) pp. 7-12.

Emrich, Wilhelm: Franz Kafka. Frankfurt 1960.

Fickert, Kurt: A Literal Interpretation of "In the Penal Colony." Modern Fiction Studies 17 (1971) pp. 31-36.

_____ Kafka's "Assistants" from the Castle. International Fiction Review 3 (Jan. 1976) pp. 3-6.

_____ Kafka's "In the Penal Colony." The Explicator 24 (Sept. 1965) item 11.

_____ The Window Metaphor in Kafka's "Trial." Monatshefte 58 (1966) pp. 345-352.

Flores, Angel, ed.: The Kafka Problem. New York 1946.

Flores, Angel and Homer Swander, ed.: Franz Kafka Today. Madison, Wisc. 1958.

Foulkes, A. P.: The Reluctant Pessimist. The Hague & Paris 1967.

Fürst, Norbert: Die offenen Geheimtüren Franz Kafkas. Heidelberg 1956.

Glicksberg, Charles I.: The Self in Modern Literature. University Park, Pa. 1963.

Gray, Ronald: Franz Kafka. Cambridge 1973.

Gray, Ronald: Kafka's Castle. Cambridge 1956.

Greenberg, Martin: The Terror of Art. New York 1965.

Hall, Calvin S. & Richard E. Lind: Dreams, Life, and Literature:
    A Study of Franz Kafka. Chapel Hill 1970.

Hatfield, Henry: Crisis and Continuity in Modern German Literature.
    Ithaca, N. Y. 1969.

Heller, Erich: The Disinherited Mind. New York 1959.

———— Franz Kafka. New York 1974.

Heller, Erich & Joachim Zeug, ed.: Franz Kafka/Dichter über ihre
    Dichtungen. München 1969.

Heller, Peter: Dialectics and Nihilism. N. p. 1966 (University of
    Massachusetts Press).

Janouch, Gustav: Gespräche mit Kafka. Frankfurt 1968.

Kuna, Franz: Franz Kafka: Literature as Corrective Punishment.
    Bloomington & London 1974.

Kuna, Franz, ed.: On Kafka: Semi-Centinary Perspectives. New
    York 1976.

Martini, Fritz: Das Wagnis der Sprache. Stuttgart 1961.

Muschg, Walter: Die Zerstörung der deutschen Literatur. München
    1961.

Neider, Charles: The Frozen Sea. New York 1962.

Neumeyer, Peter F., ed.: Twentieth Century Interpretations of
    The Castle. Englewood Cliffs, N. J. 1969.

Parry, Idris: Animals of Silence. London 1972.

Pascal, Roy: From Naturalism to Expressionism. New York 1973.

———— The German Novel. Manchester 1956.

Philippi, Klaus-Peter: Reflexion und Wirklichkeit. Tübingen 1966.

Politzer, Heinz: Franz Kafka: Parable and Paradox. Ithaca, N. Y.
    1962.

Politzer, Heinz, ed.: Franz Kafka. Darmstadt 1973.

Rogers, Robert: The Double in Literature. Detroit 1970.

Rolleston, James, ed.: Twentieth Century Interpretations of "The Trial." Englewood Cliffs, N. J. 1976.

Sheppard, Richard: On Kafka's Castle. New York 1973.

Sokel, Walter H. Franz Kafka--Tragik und Ironie. München & Wien 1964.

Tauber, Herbert: Franz Kafka. Zürich & New York 1941.

Tiefenbrun, Ruth: Moment of Torment. Carbondale & Edwardsville 1973.

Thorlby, Anthony: Kafka: A Study. London 1972.

Tymms, Ralph: Doubles in Literary Psychology. Cambridge 1949.

Wagenbach, Klaus: Franz Kafka (Eine Biographie seiner Jugend, 1883-1912). Bern 1958.

_____ Franz Kafka in Selbstzeugnissen und Bilddokumenten. Reinbek bei Hamburg 1964.

Walser, Martin: Beschreibung einer Form. München 1968.

Weinberg, Kurt: Die Travestien des Mythos. Bern & München 1963.

Wiese, Benno von: Der deutsche Roman, 2 vol. Düsseldorf 1963.

allegory 9, 40, 56, 90
Allemann, Bede 52
alter ego 28, 34, 40
Amalia (in The Castle) 72, 73
Amerika (see One Who Vanished)
Anders, Günther 78
Angst 16
ape, the (in A report to an Academy) 62
Arbeiter-Unfall-Versicherungs-Anstalt 18, 21
Artur (in The Castle) 53, 69-73, 82
Auf der Galerie (see Up in the Gallery)

Bachelor's Misfortunes, The 30
Barnabas (in The Castle) 70, 71, 82
Der Bau (see Structure, The)
Bauer, Felice 19-21, 23, 33, 34, 43, 47, 50, 51, 53, 58, 83
Die Bäume (see Trees, The)
Before the Law 33, 44, 57
Bendemann, Georg (in The Judgment) 16, 33-36, 38, 39, 41, 47,
                                    48, 50 , 59, 72, 83
Bendemann the father (in The Judgment) 33-35, 39
Beschreibung eines Kampfes (see Description of a Struggle)
Betrachtung (see Observation)
Bloch, Grete 20, 53
Block (in The Trial) 56, 85
Blumfeld an Elderly Bachelor 69, 89
Blumfeld, ein älterer Junggesell, see above
Brandenfeld, Frieda (in The Judgment) 33, 40
Bridgwater, Patrick 10, 77
Brief an den Vater (see Letter to his father)
Briefe (see Letters)
Brod, Max 9, 17-19, 23, 33, 52, 56, 61, 69, 70, 73, 75, 76, 84
Brunelda (in Amerika) 40, 42, 43, 85
Bürgel (in The Castle) 73

Captain Lanz (in The Trial) 53
Castle, The 10, 31, 53, 67, 70, 72 - 74, 84
chaplain, the (in the Trial) 56, 57
Chaplin, Charles 58

Child and the City, The 18
clothes (see symbol)
Collins, H. Platzer 41, 82
Conversation with a Drunken Man 28
Conversation with the Supplicant 27
Country Doctor, A 21, 37, 39, 49, 60-63

Delamarche (in Amerika) 40-42
Description of a Struggle 27, 28, 52
Diamant, Dora 23
dichotomy 67
Dichter 21-23, 70, 72, 74-77
dog (see symbol)
Doppelgänger (see symbol)
double (see also symbol) 41, 53, 61, 69, 74, 77, 81, 82, 85, 89

Ein Hungerkünstler (see Hunger-Artist, A)
Ein Landarzt (see Country Doctor, A)
Eine kleine Frau (see Little Woman, A)
Eine Kreuzung (see Hybrid, A)
Emrich, Wilhelm 9, 10, 15, 70, 74, 83
Erlanger (in The Castle) 72
Erstes Leid (see First Sorrow)
Erzählungen und kleine Prosa (see Stories)
execution machine (see symbol)
executioners, the (in The Trial) 58

First Sorrow 75
Flores, Angel 9
food (see symbol)
Forschung eines Hundes (see Research Project of a Dog)
Frau Grubach (in The Trial) 51
Fräulein Bürstner (in The Trial) 51-53, 55, 58
Fräulein Montag (in The Trial) 52, 55
Franz the warder (in The Trial) 50, 53, 84
Frieda (in The Castle) 67, 70-73, 83
friend in Russia, the (in The Judgment) 16, 33-35, 38, 41, 72
Frye, Northup 89
Fürst, Norbert 15, 43, 54, 67, 75

Gardena (in The Castle) 71
Giacomo (in Amerika) 43, 44

Gespräch mit dem Beter (see Conversation with the Supplicant)
Giant Mole, The 76
Glicksberg, Charles 74
Gray, Ronald 10, 67, 72, 73
Green (in Amerika) 39, 83
Grete (in Metamorphosis) 48-50
Gulliver 40

Hall and Lind 31, 81, 83-85
Der Heizer (see Stoker, The)
Henel, Heinrich 9
Henel, Ingeborg 9, 11, 28
Hesse, Hermann 11, 36, 74
Hillmann, Heinz 9
Hochzeitsvorbereitungen auf dem Lande (see Wedding Preperations
        in the Country)
Hoffmann, E. T. A. 41, 82
homosexuality 41, 42, 49, 61, 82, 83, 85
Huld (in The Trial) 54-56
Hunger-Artist, A 49, 50, 74
Hunter Gracchus, The 28, 75
Hybrid, A 76

id 36, 38-41, 44, 61, 83
impotency 61
In der Strafkolonie (see below)
In the Gallery (see Up in the Gallery)
In the Penal Colony 21, 27, 59, 60, 67
insect, the (in Metamorphosis) 41, 47 - 49

Der Jäger Gracchus (see Hunter Gracchus, The)
Jeremias (in The Castle) 69, 71-73, 82
Jesenska, Milena 21-23, 70
Josef K. (in The Trial) 37, 50-59, 67, 84, 89
Josefine die Sängerin (see below)
Josefine, The Singer 10, 75
Journals 16, 18-20, 22, 30, 33, 35, 36, 49, 51, 59
Judgment, The 16, 20, 21, 31 - 33, 36, 38, 39, 47, 48, 50, 59

K. (in The Castle) 10, 31, 37, 67-73, 82-85
Kafka, Herrmann 15-17, 21, 23, 30, 32-35, 40, 43, 83
Kafka, Julie 15, 16, 51

Kelly, John 56
Kierkegaard, Søren 56, 57, 85
Das Kind und die Stadt (see Child and the City, The)
Klamm (in The Castle) 70, 71
Klara (in Amerika) 39
Klopstock, Robert 23, 30
Kuhn, Helmut 29
Kuna, Franz 10
Kundrie 55

Leni (in The Trial) 54, 55, 67
Letter to his father 21, 23
Letters 17, 21-23, 30, 47, 59, 84
Little Woman, A 75
Löwy, Rudolf 30, 54

Mack (in Amerika) 39
magic idealism 31
manageress, the (in Amerika) 41
Mann, Thomas 11, 74
masochism 60, 62
Mendel, Josef (in Amerika) 42
Metamorphosis 20, 21, 36, 47-49, 59, 69
metaphor (see symbol)
Milena (see Jesenska, Milena)
Modern Times 58
Moore, Marianne 31
Musil, Robert 11
music (see symbol)
myth 71, 90

Nagel, Bert 9, 10
names (see symbol)
Neider, Charles 9, 41, 67, 85
New Prosecutor, The 37
Novalis 31

Observation 19, 29-31, 33
observer, the (in In the Penal Colony) 59, 60
Of Metaphors 29
officer, the (in In the Penal Colony) 59, 60
Old Commandant, the (in In the Penal Colony) 59

Olga (in The Castle) 72, 73
One Who Vanished 19, 34, 36, 40–42, 48, 67, 69, 72, 83

parable 57
Pascal, Roy 74
patient, the (in A Country Doctor) 61, 62
Paul, Jean 81
Penalties 59
Pepi (in The Castle) 73, 84
Philippi, Klaus-Peter 74
Politzer, Heinz 9, 10, 40, 60, 67, 74, 77
Pollack, Oskar 17
Pollunder (in Amerika) 39, 40, 83
Pongs, Hermann 89
Der Prozess (see Trial, The)

Raban, Eduard (in Wedding Preparations in the Country) 28, 29, 51
Die Räuber 37
Report to an Academy 62, 76
Research Project of a Dog 36, 49, 76, 85
Richard and Samuel 18
Der Riesenmaulwurf (see Giant Mole, The)
Robinson (in Amerika) 40–42
Robinson Crusoe 46 f., 53
Rogers, Robert 81, 83
Rossmann, Karl (in Amerika) 28, 37–44, 67, 83, 85

sadism 53, 60
Samsa, Gregor (in Metamorphosis) 47–49, 59, 85
Das Schloss (see Castle, The)
Schubal (in Amerika) 38
Sheppard, Richard 10, 67
Söhne (see Sons)
Sokel, Walter 9, 70
Sons 47
Sordini (in The Castle) 68, 73
Sortini (in The Castle) 68, 72, 73
Spann, Meno 9
State of Misery, The 31–35, 38, 44, 47, 60
Statue of Liberty, the 38
Steckel, Wilhelm 84
Steppenwolf, The 36, 43

Stoker, The 36, 47
Stories (and Prose Sketches) 27-29, 32, 33
Strafen (see Penalties)
Structure, The 76-78
super-ego 36, 38, 39, 44, 83
supplicant, the (in Conversation with the Supplicant) 27
symbol
      bachelor 30
      castle 59, 67, 68, 72-74, 83
      child-ghost 31-34, 38, 41, 44, 47, 61
      Clayton 43
      clothes 28, 30, 31, 84
      court 52, 53, 58
      dog 56, 59, 85, 91 f.
         aerial dogs 36, 77, 85
      Doppelgänger 11, 30, 34, 36, 41, 50, 61, 81, 85
      double figure 22, 39, 41, 58, 59, 69, 82
      drunken man 28
      execution machine 10, 59, 60, 84
      father figure 39, 41, 48
      food 49
         apple(s) 49
      marriage 29
      muse 48, 71, 75
      music 49
      Oklahoma 43
      panther 74
      penal colony 59
      names 37, 50, 52-54, 56, 68, 75
         Italian 46 f., 55
      Nature Theater 38, 43
      scapegoat 21
      surveyor 59, 67, 68
      village 68, 72, 73
      women 41, 48, 55
      wound 22, 23, 41, 49, 59, 61, 62

Tagebücher (see Journals)
Tauber, Herbert 9
Therese (in Amerika) 41, 72
Thorlby, Anthony 10
Tiefenbrun, Ruth 82

Titorelli (in The Trial) 55
Trees, The 29, 30
Trial, The 44, 50, 51, 55-60, 67, 69, 72, 83, 84, 89

Uncle Jakob (in Amerika) 38, 39, 44
Uncle Karl (in The Trial) 54
Das Unglück des Junggesellen (see Bachelor's Misfortunes, The)
Unglücklichsein (see State of Misery, The)
Up in the Gallery 31, 62, 67, 75
Das Urteil (see Judgment, The)

vocation 37, 40
Von den Gleichnissen (see Metaphors)
Vor dem Gesetz (see Before the Law)

Wagenbach, Klaus 15
Walser, Martin 9, 28
Wedding Preparations in the Country 28, 29, 51, 73
Weinberg, Kurt 54, 55, 72
Weiss, Ernst 53
Willem (in The Trial) 53, 84
Wish to be an Indian 31
Wohryzek, Julie 21
wound (see symbol)
Wunsch, Indianer zu werden (see Wish to be an Indian)